HORNCHURCH
STREETS OF HEROES

HORNCHURCH
STREETS OF HEROES

A Lasting Tribute to those who flew from
Hornchurch Aerodrome

Richard C. Smith

Mitor Publications

Published & typeset by
Mitor Publications
20 Theydon Gardens,
Rainham,
Essex
RM13 7TU
www.mitorpublications.co.uk

Copyright © Richard C. Smith 2013

ISBN 9780-9557180-3-8

Cover Design by Ian Taylor
Ian.taylor21@sky.com

Printed by Martins the Printers Limited
Sea View Works, Spittal Berwick upon Tweed TD15 1RS
www.martin-the-printers.co.uk

CONTENTS

Acknowledgements

Introduction

ACKNOWLEDGEMENTS

I would like to thank the following people who helped in many ways to bring about the publication of this book, supplying rare photographs and information on the pilots within.

Sincere thanks goes to, Lady Dorothy Bouchier in Japan, the wife of the late Cecil Bouchier, John Davies of Grub Street Publishers, David Ross, 603 'City of Edinburgh' Squadron historian and author. Andy Saunders, aviation archaeologist and author, Winston Ramsey, publisher of 'After the Battle' and many other notable books. The National Archive, Kew in London and the Imperial War Museum Photographic Archive in Lambeth

To the pilots, who all sadly have now passed away, but allowed access to their photographs, and to their families who also supplied vital information.

To my good friend Ian Taylor, who designed another excellent cover and photograph section and delivered the goods once again. To Martins the Printers Limited for producing the book, many thanks.

To my wife Kim and my son's David and Robert, for their continuous support and love. Finally to my friends, and the general public, who continue to support my work.

Richard C. Smith

INTRODUCTION

Following the closure of the wartime RAF Station at Hornchurch in July 1962, the Air Ministry sold off the land by auction to housing developers and gravel extraction companies and during the next few following years, the demolition teams nearly erased every single trace of the famous aerodrome. Apart from a few exceptions, the Officers' Mess and a few airmen's quarters which stood on the opposite side of the aerodrome there was nothing left to remind the residents of Havering of its renowned aeronautical history?

A new housing estate was planned and built on the site and it was decided by the London Borough of Havering that some of the streets, roads and avenues should be named after those gallant airmen who had served, fought and died during two world wars in their honour and memory.

A list was drawn up of those pilots, some famous and others not so well known, who would be chosen and those alive were contacted; those who had not survived the war or had since passed on, their families were also approached.

The first streets to be named were on the housing estate that lay on the Elm Park side of the main South End Road. The main street was named Mungo-Park Road and adjacent side-streets bore other pilot's names. Building around the old airfield site continued into the late 1970s, a main road named Airfield Way lead into Suttons Lane and was finally completed and more names were added up until 1984. The aerodromes old grass flight-paths which had been turned over for gravel extraction in the 1960s and 70s was now left to revert back to nature and is now the Hornchurch Country Park.

This book gives the reader a detailed account of each pilot's life and career covering their time at Hornchurch and their subsequent service within the Royal Air Force. Many became famous household names during both First and Second World Wars; others who have now mainly been forgotten in the passage of time are brought once again to the fore in this book, as a reminder to future generations of the price and pain that our countrymen paid for our freedom all those years past.

Richard C. Smith, April 2013

HORNCHURCH STREETS OF HEROES

Adnams Walk – Air Commodore Alfred Guy Adnams MiD

Alfred Guy Adnams was born on 5th November 1909, hence his middle name was chosen because of this. Little is known of his early life or where he was educated; but on 14th September 1928, he enrolled into initial officer training at the RAF Depot at Uxbridge and was appointed to a short service commission. On 1st October he was sent as a pilot-under-training to No. 5 Flying Training School and on completion of this course was posted to No. 19 Squadron. He remained with this unit until 17th December, when he was chosen to become a qualified flying instructor on the staff at No. 5 Flying Training School. So successful was Adnams in this role that he was chosen to join the staff instructors at the RAF College at Cranwell on 26th May 1931.

While serving at Cranwell, he attended a Signals Course at the Electrical and Wireless School and passed with top marks. He was then posted to RAF Hornchurch in Essex, where he became signals officer. On 1st September 1933, he was granted a permanent commission with the rank of flying officer. He remained in his post at Hornchurch until 1st February 1935, when he joined No. 208 Squadron again as a signals officer, out in the Middle East.

He returned to instructing as a flight commander with No. 4 Flying Training School in October 1937 before being posted as the officer commanding No. 6 Squadron on 17th April 1938 at Ramleh, in Palestine, later that year in September he was moved to Headquarters No. 6 (Auxiliary) Group with the role of Maintenance Liaison Officer. By this period Adnams had risen to the rank of squadron leader. In January 1939, he attended the RAF Staff College and in August was on the staff of Directorate of Operations (Home).

Following the outbreak of war in September 1939, Adnams remained in this appointment for the next year before being put on the staff of Directorate of Plans on 28th October 1940 and being promoted to wing commander. It would be nearly two years before he was promoted again, to group captain and made commanding officer at one of the front-line aerodromes on the Kent coast at RAF Manston on 1st April 1942.

Surprisingly, his time there was only brief and in July he was moved to command RAF Northolt near London. He was transferred at the beginning of January 1943, back to the aerodrome he had previously spent two years during the 1930s, he returned to command RAF Hornchurch. During his time there, the squadrons were extremely busy on offensive sweeps over northern France and escorting the American bombers on daylight raids as far as the German frontiers. Adnams was kept busy not only with the everyday running of the aerodrome, but because Hornchurch was located so near to London, it was ideally placed for important visitors to be taken and shown the latest aircraft or equipment being used by Fighter Command. Presentation Spitfires which had been funded by companies or towns were also ceremoniously unveiled in the presence of dignitaries and Adnams had to organise the smooth running of such events. Guests that visited during his time there included two royal Arabian princes, a famous Russian woman sniper who had killed over one hundred Germans and many delegates from various countries supporting the allied cause. While at Hornchurch, he was mentioned in Despatches for his outstanding work on 2nd June 1943

On 10th January 1944, Adnams time at Hornchurch came to an end and he was posted on to the staff at Air Plans Combined Operations Advice at Headquarters Combined Operations who were preparing for the invasion of the Allied forces back across the Channel into France. Adnams remained in this role right through the remainder of the war until final victory over the Nazis. He was promoted to the rank of acting Air Commodore and was made Commandant of the RAF Staff College at Haifa in Egypt on 9th August 1945. He remained at Haifa before he was given the job of Air Attaché, Rome in November 1947 and on 20th February 1951 he became Director of Operations.

His final appointment was as Air Officer Commanding, Royal Australian Air Force Land-Air Warfare School at Williamstown in New South Wales, Australia on an exchange posting on 25th February 1955. He finally retired from the service on 24th August 1957. He died in 1968.

Bader Way – Group Captain Douglas Bader KBE, CBE, DSO* DFC*

One name in this book should be instantly recognisable to most people as probably the most famous of Second World War pilots who served in the Royal Air Force. Although Douglas Bader flew operationally from RAF Hornchurch, he was never stationed there with one of the home based squadrons.

Born in St. John's Wood, London on 21st February 1910, his early infant years were spent in India, where his father served in the Civil Service, before the young Douglas was sent back to England to live with an aunty and began his education at a preparatory school at Temple Grove, Eastbourne in Sussex. He won a scholarship to St. Edwards College at Oxford, but excelled more in sports than academics.

In 1928, he won a prize cadetship to attend the RAF College at Cranwell in that September. After undertaking and completing the course in July 1930, Bader was given a commission and posted to No. 23 Squadron at Kenley on 25th August that year.

By 1931, he was chosen to represent the squadron as one of the pilots of the pair's aerobatic team for the Hendon Air Display, in which the squadron won for the third consecutive year.

It was on 14th December 1931, that tragedy struck and Bader's life would be changed forever. While on a visit to a small aero-club, and being taunted by a few civilian pilots about how RAF pilots only performed for the big shows, Bader took off in his Bristol Bulldog biplane to undertake a couple of passes over the critics below.

Unfortunately, while attempting a low roll, his aircrafts wing caught the ground and his aircraft slammed into the earth. He was seriously injured and taken immediately to hospital, where a surgeon had no option but to remove his right leg above the knee and the left just below the knee cap. His life hung in the balance for many days, but his will to live was strong and he recovered after many months in hospital.

Bader then was fitted with artificial limbs and once mobile re-joined the RAF, but it would prove to be one of the unhappiest times as he was grounded with no chance of flying again. He was finally retired from the RAF in 1933 and managed to get a job with the Asiatic Petroleum Company, but to Bader the routine of working behind a desk became a daily battle against boredom.

His luck finally changed however at the outbreak of war in September 1939. Forever the optimist, he made his way to the Air Ministry in the hope the RAF would need every pilot for the war ahead. He managed to persuade them to give him the chance to prove them wrong and on 18th October 1939 he was sent to the Central Flying School at Upavon for a flying test. Bader was successful, passing the test which was conducted by Squadron Leader R.H.A. Leigh. He was immediately commissioned back into the service as a flying officer and following a refresher course, he was posted to No. 19 Squadron based at Duxford in February 1940. The following month, he was promoted to the rank of flight lieutenant and posted to No. 222 'Natal' Squadron, also based at Duxford.

It was to be during the famous evacuation of British and Allied troops from the town and beaches of Dunkirk, that Bader's link with Hornchurch began.

Following the German Blitzkrieg advance through Belgium and France at the beginning of May 1940, the allied armies had been pushed back in disarray, following defeat after defeat. By 19th May, the British Expeditionary Force was instructed to retreat and make its way back to the port of Dunkirk and prepare to be evacuated by the Royal Navy in an operation code-named 'Dynamo'. The Royal Air Force would provide the air cover over Dunkirk and surrounding areas against attack from the German Luftwaffe. Hornchurch's squadrons were put on immediate alert to make ready to undertake patrol over the beaches. Hornchurch's home-based squadrons consisted of 54, 65 and 74, but during this period other squadrons flew into the aerodrome to use it to undertake operations across the Channel.

One of these was 222 Squadron; they arrived at Hornchurch on 28th May, led by the squadron commander, Squadron Leader 'Tubby' Mermagen, with Douglas Bader leading 'A' Flight. The squadron were in action over Dunkirk the following day, but it would not be until 1st June that Bader would claim his first enemy aircraft of the war. 222 along with 19 Squadron were ordered off at 4.30 am for the first patrols of the day. They arrived over France at 5 am and after patrolling for 30 minutes, 19 Squadron spotted a dozen or so Messerschmitt 110s at 4,500 feet. They attacked the enemy aircraft, but failed to notice the German fighters above, which came screaming down to help their comrades. On seeing this, Bader and 222 joined into the fray. Turning and twisting aircraft filled the sky. Flying Spitfire P9443, Bader latched on to a Messerschmitt Me109. His own report of the action states:

I was flying at about 3,000 feet when an Me109 appeared straight in front of me, going in the same direction and at about the same speed. The pilot must have been inexperienced as I was as he continued to stay in the same position as I shot him down.

Bader also claimed a share in the probable destruction of a Heinkel 111.

The squadron continued its operations until it withdrew from Hornchurch on 4th June and flew to Lincolnshire to the airfield at Kirton-in-Lindsey. This was Bader's only time at Hornchurch throughout the war. The following month, he was given command of No.242 Squadron at Coltishall in Norfolk, a squadron which had returned from France having suffered casualties and was now suffering low morale. The rest is history, Bader's fame continued to grow throughout 1940, courting much controversy with his approach to using the 'Big Wing' tactic during the Battle of Britain.

He led the 'Tangmere Wing' in March 1941, adding to his score of enemy aircraft destroyed. However, on 9th August while escorting a bomber raid to Bethune in Northern France, he was separated from the rest of his squadron and became involved in combat with several German fighter aircraft. Claiming a Me109 destroyed, he was himself brought down. He baled-out and on landing was captured by the Germans and became a prisoner of war. After attempting escape and becoming a difficult prisoner in various camps, he was eventually sent to the infamous Colditz Castle, where he remained until liberation at the end of the war.

During peacetime he joined Shell Oil and became their managing director of Shell's aircraft fleet and was given his own aircraft to travel overseas with. He became heavily involved with encouraging and supporting the disabled, especially young people who had lost limbs. He was awarded a CBE for his work in this field in 1956. He was awarded a Knighthood in 1976.

Douglas Bader sadly passed away on 5th September 1982 whilst he was returning home in the car driven by his wife, after attending a dinner in honour of Sir Arthur Harris, Marshal of the Royal Air Force.

Beaumont Crescent – Pilot Officer, the Honourable Walter Beaumont DFC

Born in Dewsbury, Yorkshire in 1914; the second son of Frederick and Delia Beaumont nee McNaulty. The family moved soon after to the town of Mytholmroyd, seven miles west of Halifax and here the young Walter began his education at the infant and junior Calderdale School in Scout Road. From here he progressed to the Hebden Bridge Grammar School and afterwards attended the London University and studied for a Bachelor of Science degree, which he achieved in 1934.

It was during this time that he joined the Air University Squadron and from 1937 was the very first person to join the RAF Volunteer Reserve with the No. 740000. During this period, he had become a teacher at the Enfield Grammar School and had settled in Coulsdon, Surrey with his new wife Doris Gosling, whom he married in early 1938, they had a son Michael who was born in December that year.

Beaumont was called up on 1st September 1939 and on completion of training was posted to join No. 152 Squadron based at Acklington in early 1940. The squadron moved south to Warmwell in July in No. 10 Group covering the south west. In action during the Battle of Britain, Beaumont claimed his first victories, when he shared in the shooting down of a Messerschmitt 109 and damaged two Junkers Ju88 bombers on the 12th August. He followed this success on 16th, when he claimed two Me109s destroyed and two days later two Ju87
Stuka dive-bombers and another shared 109; another Ju88 was shot down on 22nd and on 25th a further 109 was added to his increasing tally.

He shared in the shooting down of a Heinkel bomber on 27th August, but in return his own Spitfire was hit by enemy fire from A Junkers Ju88 and he was forced to ditch his aircraft and he was rescued from the sea 10-miles west of Portland. By this time he had achieved the status of 'ace pilot'

Sadly, Walter Beaumont was listed as missing in action following an operational sortie on 23rd September 1940. His aircraft, Spitfire R7016 probably crashed into the Channel, his body was never recovered and he is now remembered on the Runnymede Memorial, Panel 7. He was posthumously awarded the Distinguished Flying Cross on 22nd October 1940. He was 26 years old.

The author could not find any relevant connection to Hornchurch as to why Walter Beaumont was chosen to have his name represented with a road named after him, other than he was the first member of the Royal Air Force Volunteer Reserve and that he became a Battle of Britain ace.

Bennions Close – Squadron Leader George Bennions DFC

George Herman Bennions was born at Burslem, Stoke on Trent on 15th March 1913, and the third of five children to Edward and Mary Bennions (nee Smith). He was educated at the Longton High School. He volunteered to join the RAF as an aircraft apprentice at Halton, Buckinghamshire in January 1929 and after training passed as a leading aircraftsman engine fitter in December 1931. He was recommended for a cadetship at RAF Cranwell and undertook ab-initio flying training, but the cadetship did not come to pass.

Despite the setback, Bennions continued his flying training at Grantham, Lincolnshire with No. 3 Flying Training School and after completion was posted to No. 41 Squadron based at Khormaksar, Aden in the Middle East as a sergeant pilot. During the next few years he was promoted in rank, becoming a flight sergeant in November 1938 and was commissioned as a pilot officer on 1st April 1940. Bennions first brush with Hornchurch would come on 28th May 1940, when 41 Squadron moved south from Catterick to replace 54 Squadron who deserved a well-earned rest from operations over Dunkirk. During this period, he flew many sorties, but failed to claim any enemy aircraft.

On 8th June, 41 Squadron flew back to Catterick having being fully bloodied in combat. A month later, the Battle of Britain had begun and George Bennions luck was about to change. Over the 28th and 29th July, he claimed two Messerschmitt 109s destroyed, but he was himself shot down over Dover on 29th and was forced to crash-land his Spitfire N3264 with damaged wing flaps at Manston.

In August, he claimed the destruction of a Messerschmitt Bf110 and a further one damaged, but it would be at the height of the battle in September that Bennions would show his skill and courage as a first rate fighter pilot.

On 5th September, he claimed a Junkers Ju88 bomber destroyed, an Me109 fighter probably destroyed and a Junkers Ju 88 damaged. The following day, he claimed two further Me109s, but on the 7th his own aircraft's undercarriage collapsed on landing at Rochford aerodrome following combat. A further Me109 was despatched on 9th and a Me110 damaged on 11th, but not without injury to himself, following his own attack, he had in return suffered bullet hits to his own aircraft and felt a short sharp pain in his left foot. On landing back at Hornchurch, he observed his left shoe was full of blood caused by a shell splinter that had entered his heel. He made his way from his Spitfire and found the medical officer, who removed the splinter and then applied a few stitches to his wound. He was nevertheless flying again the following day.

On 15th September Bennions reported a further 109 destroyed as well as a Dornier 17 bomber damaged. A 109 shot down on 17th with another destroyed and a further two probably destroyed with one damaged on September 18th. Combat successes continued on 23rd with another Me109 and two more probables on 28th. His final victory came on 1st October 1940.

On this day No. 41 Squadron had seen no action during the morning and it was not until the afternoon at around 2.00 pm led by Squadron Leader Don Finlay that the squadron became involved with enemy fighters, claiming one aircraft damaged. Nine Spitfires from the squadron were vectored over Maidstone at 3.50 pm and whilst at an altitude of 30,000 feet, they spotted an enemy formation of 25 Me109s. The Spitfires dived in to attack, but could only claim one of the 109s as damaged, before the enemy headed for cloud cover.

On their return trip to Hornchurch, George Bennions had spotted some Hawker Hurricanes in trouble with Me109s. He broke formation to try and help out his fellow comrades. He latched on to the rear of one of the German fighters and fired two short bursts from his machine guns, causing it to catch fire; the German pilot quickly took to his parachute. Seconds later Bennions was attacked by a German aircraft. In his own words, he describes what happened next:

I was engaged with a few 109s just north of Brighton at about 20,000 feet, when a cannon shell exploded in the cockpit, blinding me in the left eye and damaging my right arm and leg. I could not use my right hand as the median nerve had been severed. My face and right leg were bleeding profusely, so I decided to bale-out. I disconnected the oxygen tube with my left hand and pulled out the radio plug. I then opened the canopy, lowered the side door and then rolled the aircraft to drop out. I experienced great difficulty trying to pull the parachute ripcord with my left hand, but eventually succeeded. The parachute opened with a terrific jerk causing me to pass out completely. When I regained consciousness, I had already landed and was being attended to by a farmer, Mr C. J. Shepherd; I asked him would he please inform my squadron. After emergency treatment at Horsham Base Hospital, I was transferred to the Queen Victoria Hospital at East Grinstead for plastic surgery by Sir Archie McIndoe, and thus became a member of the Guinea Pig Club.

Bennions had been very badly wounded. A cannon shell had pierced his skull and destroyed his left eye; it was a miracle that he had survived. On the very day he had been shot down his award of the Distinguished Flying Cross had been awarded.

After many months of treatment, he finally returned to duty as operations controller based at Catterick. He wanted to fly again, but was given a non-operational category, to fly on by day with a passenger in attendance.

In 1943, he was posted overseas to North Africa as a Liaison Officer for an American Fighter Group. In Sicily, he was allowed to fly convoy patrols, but was not involved in combat. Bennions was wounded again on 30th September 1943, when he suffered shrapnel wounds, when the landing craft he was on was attacked by an enemy glider bomb, which had been launched from a Dornier 217 bomber at Ajaccio in Corsica.

He was returned to Britain and spent further time at the Queen Victoria Hospital for treatment to his wounds. After the war had ended, Bennions was offered a job in Administration and Special Duties Branch of the RAF, but he decided as there would be little point in continuing without the possibility of flying, he was released from the service in 1946. He entered into civilian life and for a short while worked as a welfare officer for a building firm. He then decided to enrol on a year-long teacher training course to become a school master. He continued in this role for the next 28 years.

George Bennions passed away on 30th January 2004 at the age of 90 years.

Berry Close - Air Commodore Ronald Berry CBE, OBE, DSO, DFC*

Ronald Berry was born at 28 Kelvin Street, Hull on 3rd May 1917. His first school was Riley High and from the age of 11 years went to the Hull Technical College. After finishing college, he worked as a clerk at the St. Andrew's Engineering Company at Hull Docks; he remained there for 18 months before finding employment as a clerk working on salaries and income tax for the city treasurer's office. In 1937, after seeing an advert for the Royal Air Force Volunteer Reserve in a local paper, he applied and was successful joining the RAFVR in April 1937. Berry then undertook his flying training at weekends at the Elementary & Reserve Flying Training School at Brough, taught to fly on the Blackburn B2 biplane. It was at this time that his nickname of 'Ras' Berry began, after some person had written this on the front of his flying log-book.

With war looming, Berry was called up as a sergeant pilot during February 1939 and posted to No.66 Squadron based at Duxford; but after three weeks, he was sent back to Brough. That July, he was given a five-year commission, but due to the loss of his paperwork somewhere in the system, it would not be until December that it was finally passed. His next posting was to B Flight of No. 603 'City of Edinburgh' Squadron based at Turnhouse in Scotland on 17th October 1939. The squadron was equipped with Spitfires. Fellow pilot in the squadron, Richard Hillary wrote later in his wartime book 'The Last Enemy' his impression of Berry.

'He was short and stocky with a ruddy complexion and a mouth that was always grinning or coming out with some broad Yorkshire witticism, which was impossible to answer. He sported a heavy black moustache, which induced me to call him the organ-grinder. Even on the blackest days he radiated an infectious good-humour.'

His first taste of action came on 7th December 1939, when along with other members of the squadron engaged a formation of Heinkel bombers, damaging at least two of the raiders. Ras Berry's first confirmed enemy claim came on 3rd July 1940, when at 2.05 pm, Berry flying as part of Green Section of the coast of Montrose sighted a lone Junkers Ju88.

As they approached the enemy aircraft, it took evasive action and headed for a cloud bank. Berry and Pilot Officer Stapleton were ordered to stay above cloud in case the German reappeared, while Flying Officer Carbury followed the aircraft into the clouds. Suddenly the German appeared out of the cloud and Berry and Stapleton attacked the aircraft firing short bursts. The German bomber decided enough was enough and jettisoned his bomb load and tried to make his escape. The three Spitfires pressed home their attacks and the bomber now badly damaged began to lose height before finally crashing into the North Sea.

With the Battle of Britain now in its second month and with squadrons hard pressed and tired from the continuous fighting in mainly No. 11 Group, south-east of England, 603 Squadron received orders to move south to Hornchurch on 17th August and finally took off on 27th at 11 am.

Arriving at Hornchurch 'Ras' Berry was soon in the thick of the action, the following day he claimed an Me109 destroyed and another damaged; on 31st August he had further success when he destroyed a further three 109s. By the end of the battle in October, he had claimed 8 destroyed, 5 probable destroyed and 6 damaged. Berry received the award of the DFC on 25th October 1940. His citation for the DFC read:

Pilot Officer Berry has personally destroyed six enemy aircraft and assisted in the destruction of several others. Through innumerable engagements with the enemy, he has shown the greatest gallantry and determination in pressing home his attacks at close range. The skill and dash with which this officer has led his section have done much to assure their successes.

His final claim for 1940 came on 23rd November, when he shot down an Italian Fiat Cr42 biplane, in one of only two small token raids mounted by the Italian Air Force against Britain during the entire war. He was promoted to 'A' Flight towards the end of January 1941 and then sent up to Scotland for a rest period, then given the role as a Fighter Controller at Turnhouse. By December, he had been promoted to the rank of squadron leader and by February had been given a new squadron to command, No.81 also based at Turnhouse.

The squadron's main role was to protect convoy shipping and this continued up until May 1942, they then received orders to move south, to Hornchurch again, to fly combat sweeps over northern France. Ras Berry continued to add to his score during this period, before receiving the news that he would take his squadron via Gibraltar to North Africa for 'Operation Torch' to cover the Anglo-American landings in French North Africa.

His squadron of Spitfires was the first unit to arrive at Maison Blanche airfield at the start of the operations. During this period of combat he added another three and four shared enemy aircraft destroyed.

He was promoted further in January 1943, by being given command of 322 Wing until the end of the campaign in Tunis in May 1943. For his outstanding leadership and success he was awarded a Bar to his DFC in February 1944 and a further award of the Distinguished Service Order that June. Posted back to Britain from operations, he was sent to a Spitfire Operational Training Unit at Kirton in Lindsey, Lincolnshire as Wing Commander Flying; from there he was sent to the Army Staff College and the Fighter Leaders School. At war's end, he was sent to RAF Tangmere in Sussex to form the Central Fighter Establishment. Post war, he remained in the service and held various appointments including Wing Commander Flying at RAF Wittering on Valiant jet bombers during the mid-1950s.

He became a Group Captain Ops Bomber Command in 1959 and final rank of Air Commodore on 1st January 1966. His other awards included an OBE in 1946 and a CBE in 1965. Following his retirement in 1969, he lived out his retirement in Hornsea, a small seaside resort town on the Humberside coast. His final tally for enemy aircraft stands at 14 and 10 shared destroyed, 9 probables, 17 damaged, 7 destroyed on the ground. Ronald Berry died aged 83 on 13th August 2000.

Bouchier Walk - Air Vice-Marshal Sir Cecil 'Boy' Bouchier
KBE, CBE, OBE, CB, DFC

Cecil Bouchier was born on 14th October 1895, the son of Arthur and Florence who managed the Clarence Hotel in Palmerston Street in Southsea, Sussex. He was educated at Chichester Grammer School, but following the death of his father at the age of forty-nine from tuberculosis, the owners of the hotel moved in a new manager and with no provision left for his family by the father, the Bouchier's were practically penniless.

The family then moved to Stoke Newington in North London where Cecil attended the Stamford Hill Collegiate School. It was while here that one of the boys whose father was a chairman at the Tottenham Hotspur Football Club and invited him to come and see the team during a home match. It was a great thrill for the young Cecil and he became a fan of the club which continued throughout his life. The stay at Stoke Newington was to be only brief and the family moved down south to Farnham in Surrey to a small cottage named 'Clovelly'. Here he continued his education at a small school called St. Polycarps; his mother having to take in a lodger to pay the bills.

He remained at the school until the age of fourteen; to take up a position as a junior ledger clerk at the Junior Army and Navy Stores at Aldershot. His mother received an offer from an old acquaintance, the offer of a job for Cecil to join a company named F. Sanders Stark & Company based in London, which dealt in wholesale items.
Young Cecil packed his belongings and headed for the city, where one of his roles was as a salesman for the company.

His life continued at the same pace until on 4th August 1914, when the world was plunged into conflict with the outbreak of the First World War. He immediately decided that he would volunteer for King and Country and went over to the recruiting office in a street off the Marylebone Road. After waiting for two hours, he was seen by a doctor and given the once over, but was rejected due to his small height. Later during the war, as casualties mounted on a rapid scale, the regulations for recruits were very much less critical. However the following year in March 1915, he tried his hand again, this time with the Honourable Royal Artillery Company, whose horse-drivers were men of much smaller frame than the main army. He passed and was enrolled and given a new silver shilling, what was then called 'taking the King's Shilling.' He packed his belongings and headed for the barracks at Armoury House in the City of London; here he was taught to march, rifle drill and how to load and fire the 15-pounder field guns.

He was then taught how to ride a horse at Preece's indoor riding school at Fulham. By early spring, along with twenty other drivers and gunners, Bouchier was posted overseas and sent to Egypt to protect the Suez Canal and was billeted at Kantara, midway between Port Said and Ismailia to protect against the threat from the Turkish Army. He remained in Egypt and saw action several times against the enemy.

During one period in 1917, Bouchier frequently saw the Royal Flying Corps biplanes in action in the skies above him and witnessed a number of dogfights; he became fascinated by the thought of flight and the possibility that he may be able to transfer to this new service, away from the dirt and dust and misery on the ground. At the first opportunity to arise, he asked his Battery Commander Major Eugster for transfer to the RFC. When Eugster asked, why not a commission in the artillery? Bouchier replied that he wanted to learn to fly and that they needed small lighter weight men for their aircraft. The major could not disagree and sent off a recommendation and wished him good luck.

By August 1917, Bouchier had received a letter that informed him he had been provisionally accepted into the RFC and that he should make his way to Zeitoun, near Cairo to undertake an officer's commission course. On completion and passing the course, he was sent to the School of Military Aeronautics in Heliopolis which had an airfield. Learning the rudiments of flight, aero-engines, he was then sent to Ismailia with other cadets to learn to fly. Here he undertook instruction on the Maurice Farman Shorthorn and after a week of dual flying with an instructor and only four hours in the air, he was asked to go solo. Having been awarded his wings, he was given his commission as a 2nd Lieutenant and given the job of instructing other pupils at the flying training School at Amria.

During the summer of 1918, Bouchier applied for transfer back to Britain and posting to France to get into the action on the western front. This was approved and on arriving back in England was then sent to RAF Shoreham on an instructor's refreshers course. He was graded A1 and then posted to the Royal Naval Air Service flying training school at Fairlop in Essex. Here he flew the single-seat Sopwith Camel and Pup fighter aircraft. With the end of the war in Europe looming and still no sign of going to France, Bouchier applied for service in North Russia to fly in a small RAF unit for the Czarist White Russian Army against the Bolshevik Red Army following the 1917 revolutionary uprising.

Based at Lumbshi near Lake Onega, the facilities were basic and rough, but fortunately the weather was fairly warm during spring and very hot in the summer. Bouchier flew on several bombing missions against the communists, but the advance of the Red Army continued and reports that some loyal Russians had changed sides and murdered their British officers was unnerving. Finally, Bouchier and the rest of the RAF detached to Russia were ordered to make their way to Murmansk and return to Britain, the Russian campaign was lost.

On his return to England, he was notified of the award of the Distinguished Flying Cross on 18th November for his services in Russia and given a permanent commission as a flying officer within the Royal Air Force on 2nd December 1919. His citation for the DFC read:

A very skilful pilot of marked initiative and courage. Has been brought to notice on many occasions for the determination shown in his attacks. His methods are somewhat original. By flying low, parallel with and behind the enemy's lines, stampeding convoys and destroying wagons, he has caused the greatest confusion amongst the enemy, to the great advantage of our own forces. Flying Officer Bouchier is a highly competent reconnaissance officer.

His next posting was as an instructor at RAF Thetford, but this was only a brief stay, for he was then sent abroad once more to India in January 1920, to join No. 28 Squadron at Ambala, in the Punjab region. He was posted again that November to help re-form No. 1 Squadron based at Risalpur on the North-West Frontier, their role to back up the army in defence against unruly tribes causing revolt in that region.

With the coming of aircraft the uprisings lessened, due to the fear that the tribes had of being bombed and their villages destroyed. During his time here, Bouchier contracted Dengue fever and jaundice, but following his recovery he returned to England in 1922 and was told he had been selected to become a test pilot at the Royal Aircraft Establishment at Farnborough commanded by Squadron Leader Roderick Hill. Here he undertook various test flights on experimental aircraft including the Sopwith Snipe. It was during this time that he met his future wife Gladys Dorothy Sherwood.

After three years in this position, Bouchier ended his time as a test pilot in January 1926 and given the rank of flight lieutenant, was sent to No. 41 Squadron at RAF Northolt, just west of London. Here he remained for the next three years and on 23rd July 1927, he married his fiancée Gladys at St James Church, Hampton Hill, spending their wedding night at the Waldorf Hotel. The next year, she gave birth to his Son Derek on 21st July 1928. During his time with 41 Squadron he participated in the annual Hendon Air Display Pageants and the Sir Philip Sassoon Trophy in which Bouchier's 'B' Flight won for stunting in formation.

The following year, he was once more posted overseas, back to Egypt as a test pilot to Aboukir, near Alexandria, but within eight months he was given orders to attend the RAF Staff College at Andover on 20th January 1930. After a year of intensive studying,

Bouchier passed the course and was given his first staff job to RAF Headquarters in New Deli.

He spent the next three and half years here and during this time was prominent in helping to form the beginnings of the Royal Indian Air Force and finally became its commander. He was promoted to squadron leader and was awarded an OBE for his outstanding work. Bouchier was ordered back to Britain and after reporting to the Air Ministry in London was appointed commander of No. 54 Squadron at RAF Hornchurch on 23rd August 1936. The squadron was using Gloster Gauntlet biplanes, but within a year they had been re-equipped with the new Gloster Gladiator, the first RAF Biplane to have a fully enclosed cockpit canopy. During his time with the squadron, Bouchier was able to produce the design for the squadron's own official crest under the guidance of a Mr Heaton-Armstrong, the Chester Herald. Along with the crest, he also designed the official squadron neck tie.

In March 1938, he was promoted to the rank of wing commander and appointed in Charge of Operations at No. 11 Fighter Group, Uxbridge. On his arrival, he noticed how the work now being carried out seemed to point to the threat of war becoming more inevitable with Germany. One of his main responsibilities prior to war breaking out was to ensure that 11 Group operations ran efficiently. Air Defence exercises were organised to test the system of communications between ground control and aircraft in the air.

War finally came on 3rd September 1939 and two days later, Bouchier while in his office at 11 Group, was notified he had been promoted to rank of group captain. In early December, he was asked by Air Marshal Leslie Gossage whether he would like to take command of a sector fighter station. Gossage ran a couple of names past him, Tangmere for instance in the lovely Sussex countryside near the coast. Bouchier replied that he would prefer to go to Hornchurch, where he had commanded 54 Squadron and if the enemy did attack London, he would be in the thick of it. He took up his position at Hornchurch on New Year's Eve 1939.

During his first few weeks at the aerodrome, many things had to be organised; not only here, but at the two forward airfields, which Bouchier was also in control over, at Rochford near Southend and at Manston on the Kent coast. Work was undertaken to construct dispersal huts around the perimeter track of the airfields for the pilots to use during daylight operations and remain there on 'Readiness' to await the order to take-off. Sandbag aircraft enclosures were also built to protect the Spitfire aircraft.

Another measure which Bouchier had installed was the use of a Tannoy loudspeaker system at various points around the aerodrome; he would be able to talk and inform his service personnel in what was happening on the ground and keep morale up in times of battle conditions, so everybody felt they were part of a team.

Throughout 1940, Bouchier kept the aerodrome in top condition, ensuring that his ground-staff and pilots needed for nothing. During the Dunkirk evacuation, the Hornchurch squadrons who returned exhausted sortie after sortie over the Channel, would be visited on their return by Bouchier to find how they had fared and would give them a 'well done' and get to the Mess for something to eat.' He was also on hand to proudly introduce five of his pilots to King George VI who arrived in a surprise visit to Hornchurch on 27th June 1940, to award medals for courage against the enemy.

Throughout that year, Bouchier had seen his aerodrome suffer heavy casualties in the air-fighting and bombing attacks which had left the flight-path littered with craters, but at no time had the aerodrome become non-operational.

Come December 1940, the telephone rang at Bouchier's office at Hornchurch; a call from Air Vice-Marshal Trafford Leigh-Mallory, the new commander of 11 Group, informing him that he wanted Bouchier to return as Operations Officer, Headquarters 11 Group; he accepted the job. He remained in this post until December 1941, when he was given command of the aerodrome at RAF Kenley, once again serving at a fighter station that was now taking the fight to the enemy in northern Europe.

In January 1942, He was again promoted to become Deputy Director of Fighter Operations at the Air Ministry and then Senior Air Staff Officer at Headquarters No.13 (Fighter) Group in early 1943; he was then sent to No. 11 Group in the same capacity on 14th June that year. He remained firmly in this role until the war against Germany was nearly over.

At the beginning of April 1945, he was contacted by Air Marshal Sir Hugh Saunders who at that time was Air Member for Personnel at Air Ministry. He asked him if he would accept the post of commander of 221 Group in Burma with the rank of Air Vice-Marshal. Bouchier reluctantly accepted with the thought of again having to leave his family behind. 221 Group was giving air-support to General 'Bill' Slim's 14th Army as they continued their push to drive the Japanese forces out of Burma, having won a decisive victory at Imphal. The conditions on his arrival were harrowing with a number of officers and headquarters staff laid sick with malaria, dysentery and scrub typhus; he immediately took matters in hand and organised better hygiene and that every person was issued and slept under a mosquito net and that all windows and doors be fitted likewise.

On 14th August, the Japanese surrendered following the dropping of the Atomic bombs on Hiroshima and Nagasaki. On 23rd August, Bouchier received a radio-message that high-ranking officers of the Japanese armed services wished to come to Rangoon by aircraft and surrender. He issued back instructions that the aircraft should be painted white with Red Cross markings on it and that it was to proceed to Pegu airfield, where it would be met by an escort of Spitfires and taken to Mingaladon Airfield at Rangoon.

On their arrival, Bouchier accepted their initial surrender on behalf of the Supreme Allied Commander South-East Asia and handed them over as high-ranking prisoners to await a meeting with Lieutenant General Browning, Chief of Staff to Lord Louis Mountbatten. Following the Japanese surrender in August and the American and British forces taking control over the country, Bouchier was appointed

Air Officer Commanding, British Commonwealth Air Forces of Occupation on 1st October 1945.

After spending three years in this role, he was finally posted back to England and appointed as commander of No.21 Flying Training Group, its headquarters at Swinderby, 10-miles southwest of Lincoln.

During the early part of 1949, he decided to retire from the RAF; but no sooner had he been released from the service, when he was asked by Sir Norman Kipping, Director General of the Confederation of British Industries, if he would accept the position as their Far East Representative in Tokyo.

In this new job, Bouchier's reputation within the CBI was well respected and he looked forward to a rewarding career within commerce; but this was to end abruptly on 25th June 1950, when North Korea invaded South Korea and war between the communist army and the forces of the United Nations began.

Bouchier was re-instated back to the Active List and because of his Far East experience; he was the ideal candidate to act as British Liaison Officer to the UN Commander-in-Chief, General Douglas MacArthur, serving in this capacity throughout the Korean War. During this time, Bouchier had to keep the Chiefs of Staff and Prime Minister Winston Churchill, updated daily on events taking place in Korea by sending coded reports. Churchill is reported to have stated *'I like Bouchier's stuff.'* Following hostilities in Korea, he returned to Britain and returned to his family and civilian life.

Bouchier's connection with the Royal Air Force continued, when he became one of the main principle people involved in raising money to have the church of St. Clement Danes in the Strand rebuilt to become the Church of the Royal Air Force. The building, which was designed by Christopher Wren in 1680, was nearly destroyed during the Blitz in 1941. The appeal to raise money was an outstanding success and the church was rebuilt and officially re-consecrated on 19th October 1958 in the presence of Her Majesty, Queen Elizabeth.

Following the death of his wife in 1964, he remarried in 1968 to

Dorothy Britton, a composer and writer, who he had met previously while serving in Japan. They lived in Yokohama, but returned to live in Worthing, Sussex in 1977. Cecil Bouchier died on 15th June 1979.

Boulter Gardens – Flight Lieutenant John Clifford Boulter DFC

John Clifford Boulter was born in Barnes, London in 1913. In March 1933, he was placed on the Reserve of Air Force Officers and received a commission as a pilot officer. He relinquished his commission in April 1936 on being granted a short service commission in the RAF. He undertook his flying training at 7 FTS at Peterborough from 18th April and on completion was posted to No. 1 Squadron based at RAF Tangmere in Sussex on 25th October that year. He was posted to the newly reformed 72 Squadron at Church Fenton on 23rd March 1937 and remained with them until 6th October 1939, when he was sent to join Spitfire Squadron No. 603 Squadron at Turnhouse in Scotland.

His first taste of combat was on 16th October, whilst flying with Flying Officer Rushmer and Wynne-Powell; he became separated from his Section, but stumbled across and fired on a Heinkel He111 bomber, flying east of Aberdour. The results of his attack were not known as the enemy aircraft headed into cloud and was not seen again

On 20th March 1940, Boulter was hospitalised following an accident which saw him collide on landing with an Airspeed Oxford at Montrose Airfield in Spitfire L1022.

He headed south to Hornchurch with the squadron during August 1940 and was immediately thrown into the thick of action. On 29th, he claimed a Messerschmitt 109 destroyed, but was himself slightly wounded when a bullet entered the cockpit. His report read:

Whilst on patrol with 603 Squadron I noticed a formation of Me109 aircraft above and to the front. I informed the leader of 603 of their presence and turned to intercept them. As I did so I received a bullet

24

in the cockpit, distracting my attention from my target. When trying to re-join my squadron, I saw five Me109s and engaged one of them. It broke away and I was able to carry out a quarter attack, causing a trail of grey-white smoke or vapour to pour out from the under surfaces.

Boulter had continued success against the enemy; on 11th September, he damaged a Henkel bomber, the 14th another Me109 destroyed, 17th a share in a 109 destroyed. On 23rd, he destroyed another 109 and damaged one other on 30th September. In October, he claimed a further two Messerschmitts on 2nd and 12th and a final 109 on 17th November. He destroyed an Italian Fiat CR-42 over the Channel on 23rd November.

On 6th December 1940, he was awarded the Distinguished Flying Cross. His citation reads:

This officer has continuously been engaged on active operations since October 1940. He is an excellent and determined leader, and his coolness and initiative have enabled him to destroy at least five enemy aircraft and share in the destruction of others.

The squadron headed back to Scotland on 17th December to RAF Drem. He was tragically involved in an aircraft accident on 17th February 1941, when his Spitfire was struck by a Hawker Hurricane fighter as he was about to take-off. He was critically injured and died of his injuries a week later, aged 28. He was buried in Dirleton Cemetery, East Lothian.

Broadhurst Walk– Air Chief Marshal Sir Harry Broadhurst, GCB, KCB, KBE, CB, DSO* DFS* AFC

Harry Broadhurst was born on 28th October 1905 at Frimley, Surrey. His father, also named Harry had served as a regular officer in the South Lancashire Regiment and was the Regimental Sergeant Major for many years. Harry was educated at the Portsmouth Grammar School from 1915 until 1922. After finishing his education, he entered into employment as an assistant to a surveyor and also spent a short time in the Territorial Army, joining on 21st May 1925, attaining the rank of 2nd Lieutenant in the 2nd Hampshire Heavy Brigade, Royal Artillery. On 1st October 1926, against his father's wishes, he resigned his commission and volunteered to join and train as a pilot in the RAF. It was during his early days with the RAF, that Broadhurst met and courted Doris Kathleen French. Her father was a leather wholesaler in Portsmouth.

On completion of his flying training and gaining his wings on 8th August 1927, he was given a short service commission and posted to his first squadron, No. 11 (Bomber) Squadron based at Netheravon, Wiltshire on 3rd April 1928, as a pilot officer. The squadron was sent overseas on 29th December 1929 on the HMT 'Nevassa,' arriving at Risalpur on 22nd January 1929. It was while in India that he and his fiancée decided to marry and did so in the St Thomas Cathedral, Bombay on 19th October 1929.

In 1931, his squadron flew many operations over the north-west frontier using Horsley and Wapiti biplanes and it was while undertaking action against rebellious tribes on the frontier that Broadhurst was to receive a Mentioned in Despatches award on 26th June.

When the tribes did go on to the attack, the pilots would first fly over the rebel villages, warning the inhabitants by dropping leaflets, telling them that the RAF would be back later that day to bomb the village; this was done to prevent women and children being killed.

He and his family returned to the United Kingdom in late 1931, with his next posting to No. 41 Squadron flying Bristol Bulldog aircraft, stationed at RAF Northolt. Here he undertook air-firing exercises at Sutton Bridge and became the top scorer of the competition with 133 hits achieved. In 1933, he was posted once more and undertook a flying boat course at RAF Calshot on 18th September. After finishing the course in November, he was sent to 19 Squadron as a flight commander at RAF Duxford.

Broadhurst's flying skills were soon noted by his commanding officer and he was soon asked to join and train in the squadron's aerobatic team. After nearly a year with 19 Squadron, he was sent to RAF Headquarters at Ismailia, Egypt to give instruction on air-to air firing at No. 4 Flying Training School. On his return from Egypt, He went back immediately to 19 Squadron on 9th December 1934. Here he continued as before and took back his role in the aerobatic team, which soon became the RAF's top display team and one of the top attractions at the Hendon Air Pageant and Empire Air Day displays at various airfields around the country.

During his time with the squadron, he had also won for three consecutive years the Brooke-Popham Trophy, which was awarded to the winner of the competition for best air firing. For his outstanding ability and achievements in flying, Broadhurst was awarded the Air Force Cross on 1st February 1937. He was promoted to squadron leader on 1st July and given a job on the Personnel Staff of No.2 Headquarters (Bomber) Group based at Andover on 2nd September 1937; he left this position to go on a course at the RAF Staff College, also at Andover, but returned to Headquarters Bomber Command in a temporary position until early October.

After completing a course at RAF Cranwell in December 1938, he was delighted to find he was given command of No.111 (Fighter) Squadron who were based at RAF Northolt, near London; the squadron being equipped with Hawker Hurricane Mk Is.

With war clouds looming in Europe, the RAF was now hastily preparing its men and squadrons. Many hours were spent practising the standard RAF fighter tactics and battle formations should the conflict become reality. When war was finally declared in September 1939, 111 Squadron spent the first few weeks flying shipping patrols without seeing a single enemy aircraft. On 27th October, the squadron was sent north to Acklington, here they shared the aerodrome with 607 and 152 Squadrons.

It was not until the morning of 29th November, that the squadron saw and destroyed their first enemy aircraft, the honour going to none other than Harry Broadhurst. Leading 'A' Flight, he sighted a Heinkel 111 at 8.25 am, about eight miles east of Alnwick, flying at around 4,000 feet. Firing at a range from 400 to 150 yards, Broadhurst's guns poured bullets into the bombers fuselage and it began to go into a dive before plunging into the icy North Sea.

Although the squadron had claimed their first victory of the war, most of the time it remained fairly quiet, except for the odd German reconnaissance aircraft venturing over the North Sea. As 1940 started, Broadhurst was awarded the Distinguished Flying Cross on 2nd January for his work on operations and later that month he was promoted as acting Wing Commander and posted to Headquarters No.11 Group for Air Staff Training.

At the beginning of May, the German Blitzkrieg began with a lightning attack through Holland, Belgium and France; the allied armies had been caught totally unprepared for such a decisive and breath-taking advance.

On 10th May, Wing Commander Broadhurst was posted to take command of RAF Coltishall in Norfolk. As the situation in Europe worsened and with the British Expeditionary Force and the French in full retreat, by 18th May, Broadhurst was given orders to take command of No. 60 Wing based at Vitry in France. On 20th May, he claimed his second victory while leading a section of Hurricanes from 79 Squadron and 213 Squadron, while over Arras at an altitude of 15,000 feet they encountered a formation of four Messerschmitt 110 fighter-bombers with a further 25 enemy machines above at 18,000 feet. During the action, Broadhurst claimed one destroyed. On return to Merville, he received instructions to evacuate the airfield and destroy any unserviceable aircraft and get the remaining Hurricanes to head back home across the Channel.

As he flew back to England, he was harried and shot up by four Me110s. He managed to evade the enemy fighters and landed back at Northolt, his aircraft riddled with bullet holes and the oil tank damaged. A week later, Broadhurst collected his repaired Hurricane P2823 and had it painted black, with his initials HB painted red on the side of the fuselage. He then returned to Coltishall to resume his role as station commander, but two days later on 28th May, he was given command of RAF Wittering in Cambridgeshire.

By the start of the Battle of Britain in July 1940, Broadhurst had under his command three squadrons, No's 23, 229, 226. Throughout August, the squadrons at Wittering spent most of their time either undertaking local tactical exercises or night patrols over local areas, including a two-squadron patrol over Duxford on 24th September. During this period of intense action down in the south-east of England in Essex and Kent, Broadhurst no doubt felt left out of the fighting that was taking place. He later commented that he could not be considered as a Battle of Britain pilot, as he was in 12 Group at Wittering away from the heavy fighting.

On 20th December 1940, he was given notice of his new command, the fighter station at RAF Hornchurch in Essex. He recalls:

I was given command of Hornchurch, but my relief at Wittering had not arrived to take over; so I didn't take over at Hornchurch until the first week in January 1941, when we were just about to start the offensive sweeps over to France against Jerry.

After arriving at his new command, Broadhurst went out of his way to meet and talk to the pilots that he would lead in the air.

On 25th February 1941, during the early afternoon, he led 611 Squadron on an offensive sweep over Dunkirk and sighted six Me109s at 12,000 feet south-west of Gravelines. He led his Spitfires down into attack and during this combat claimed one of the enemy machines destroyed and another damaged. Throughout February and March, the Hornchurch Wing continued to venture inside the French coast, escorting small forces of light-bombers to attack German installations, airfields and army bases. Broadhurst again inspired his pilots and as usual led from the front.

On 21st June, a signal arrived at Hornchurch conveying to Harry Broadhurst the news that he had been awarded the Distinguished Service Order. One of his fellow commanders and friend was Basil Embury who was in charge of RAF Wittering; he wrote to Broadhurst:

My Dear Broady

A line to congratulate you very heartily on the award of the DSO. I was delighted to hear of it, as you know the jolly fine job of work you have been putting up at Hornchurch. I know that your leadership and personal example have been an inspiration, not only to your own unit, but to Fighter Command.

He continued to lead the Hornchurch Wing and inspire the people around him and during this period claimed 8 enemy aircraft destroyed, 6 probables and 4 damaged.

On 13th October 1941, Broadhurst left his command at Hornchurch and was sent on a goodwill lecture tour of the United States of America. This had been organised by the Air Ministry who had selected six distinguished airmen representing Bomber and Fighter Command. Following the month long tour, he returned to take up his command at Hornchurch. In December, he was awarded a bar to add to his DSO medal for the amount of enemy aircraft he had destroyed.

He continued to fly operations with the Wing until 11th May 1942, when he received notification of his appointment as Deputy Senior Air Staff Officer at 11 Group. It was a sad farewell to the officers and personnel of RAF Hornchurch who he had commanded and fought with over 17 months.

During the Allied raid against the port town of Dieppe on 19th August 1942, Broadhurst was again heavily involved in the air-planning to give air-support over Dieppe against the Luftwaffe. So much so, that he borrowed a Spitfire from Hornchurch and flew four reconnaissance sorties over the beachhead that day, providing valuable first-hand information. During his first trip he also shot down a Focke-Wulf 190. He finally landed back at Northolt at 7.00 pm from his fourth sortie having flown a total of 8 ½ hours in a day. For his outstanding contribution to operations, he was awarded a bar to his DFC on 16th September 1942.

He remained at 11 Group until he received notification of his appointment as Senior Air Staff Officer to Desert Air Force on 31st October 1942. Soon after the Battle of El Alamein, he arrived at the Headquarters of Desert Air Force, under the command of Air Marshal Arthur Coningham. The late Air Vice-Marshal and top scoring British Ace of WW2, J.E. Johnnie Johnson recalled Broadhurst's contribution when he became commander of Desert Air Force:

He proved to be an outstanding commander and leader, and he soon gained the full confidence of the leader of the 8th Army, General Bernard Montgomery. Before 'Broady' had arrived on the scene most fighter-bomber pilots had made the majority of their attacks whenever they saw opportunity targets during flights over the battlefield. Broadhurst however, thought his pilots could provide better support for the army chaps, if they knew more about the ground battle and the whereabouts of enemy tanks and armour. In other words, he wanted more planned set-piece attacks and less staffing of opportunity targets. RAF controllers in armoured cars, situated with the forward troops, and in radio contact achieved this with the squadrons already in the air, awaiting instructions from the ground.

He soon became Air Officer Commanding Desert Air Force and was promoted to the rank of acting Air Vice-Marshal, the youngest officer in the RAF to rise to that rank at the age of 38, on 31st January 1943.

By 12th May 1943, the remaining German forces in North Africa had been surrounded and forced to surrender. Nearly a quarter of a million Axis prisoners were captured. The war in the desert was over. The next operation in which he would be involved was the invasion of Sicily. The operation took 38 days to secure the island and fell to the Allies on 17th August 1943. Following the fall of Sicily, Broadhurst was involved with the invasion of Italy, but during March 1944, he was posted back to Britain to take command of No.83 Group 2nd Tactical Air Force as the build-up and preparations for the invasion of France were now under way. He was highly delighted to learn of the next award bestowed upon him, when on 11th April 1944, he was given the United States of America's Legion of Merit confirmed by President Franklin D. Roosevelt.

On 6th June 1944, the Allies landed on the beaches of Normandy, Broadhurst's squadrons covered the troops as they slowly advanced inland of the beachhead. By 25th July, the American & British Divisions had smashed through the German lines and into more open countryside. The German army had been pushed into an area known as the Falaise Gap and were now threatened with complete encirclement by the Allied armies.

The retreating army was caught out in the open by Broadhurst's rocket firing Typhoons and it became a killing field. After the battle was over, the Germans had lost 60,000 men killed or captured 500 tanks and over 5,000 vehicles.

On 25th August, French, British and American forces entered Paris. By January 1945, the German Luftwaffe launched their last ditch attempt against the Allied Air Forces airfields in France, Belgium and Holland in an operation code-named 'Bodenplatte.' The surprise attack caught many of Broadhurst's aircraft on the ground and many were destroyed, but the Germans suffered terrible casualties and lost over 300 aircraft and valuable pilots they could ill afford. The Allies lost 200 aircraft, but these were soon replaced.

When war ended in May 1945, Broadhurst remained in the RAF to pursue his career. For his outstanding service to the country, he was made a Knight of the British Empire (KBE) on 5th July 1945. In September, he was appointed Air Officer in Charge of Administration at Fighter Command and in August 1947 became Air Officer Commander of Headquarters 61 Group. On 1st July 1949, he was promoted in rank to Air-Vice-Marshal and on 1st February 1950 appointed as Senior Air Staff Officer to Headquarters British Armed Forces Overseas, before being given the position of Commander-in-Chief of 2nd Tactical Air Force in Germany on 3rd December 1953 as acting Air Marshal. In January 1956, he was appointed by the Air Council to become Air Officer Commander-in-Chief of Bomber Command, now aged 50. When he arrived at his new command, he was totally unimpressed and remarked:

To be utterly frank, I was appalled at the tedious way they were still behaving. Bomber Command was still back in WW2. Aircraft were taking up to six hours to get airborne. I therefore decided to put a 'jerk' into the command by bringing in a few fighter people like myself to get things moving faster.

Broadhurst decided to introduce the 'Quick Reaction Alert' procedure, which was being used by the RAF jet fighter squadrons. He now commanded Britain's RAF nuclear cold war deterrent against the Russian threat from the Eastern Block. Later that year, he provided air support during the Suez Crisis.

In 1956, a new aircraft came into service with the RAF, the delta-winged Avro Vulcan and Harry Broadhurst was selected to go on a worldwide tour of Commonwealth countries with one of the new aircraft Vulcan XA897. After successful trips to Australia and New Zealand, they headed home to Britain, where a large welcoming party of VIPs would meet them on landing at Heathrow airport on 1st October.

However, the weather turned bad with hardly any visibility and on the aircraft's final approach to land, Broadhurst who was seated in the co-pilots seat noticed they were too low. He told the pilot, Squadron

Leader Howard to pull up, but it was too late and the aircraft hit the ground. Howard and Broadhurst managed to fire off their ejection seats and were shot clear of the doomed aircraft, but the remaining crew of four all perished. Howard landed unhurt, but Broadhurst suffered fractures to his feet and back. After time off to recover from the incident, he resumed his career and was promoted to Air Chief Marshal on 14th February 1957.

On 29th May 1959, he was appointed Commander, Allied Forces Central Europe and remained in this post until 1st March 1961, when he voluntarily retired from the Royal Air Force after 35 years. Soon after his retirement from the service, he was asked to join A.V. Roe and Company as their managing director and from there in 1965; he became deputy managing director of Hawker Siddeley Aviation Limited until retiring in 1976.

Although throughout his busy service life he had very little time for relaxation, he did have numerous hobbies, these included sailing, cricket and rugby and he was also keen on classical music and opera.

On 5th July 1983, Harry Broadhurst returned to Hornchurch once more, he arrived as guest of honour to unveil a memorial stone within the grounds of the R.J. Mitchell School, on the site where once stood RAF Hornchurch. After the official opening, Sir Harry met with many old wartime comrades, whom he had commanded at the aerodrome. The author was privileged to meet and interview Sir Harry at his home in 1995. Although in the twilight of his life, he could still tell a darn good yarn and possessed an incredibly dry wit.

Harry Broadhurst peacefully passed away on 29th September 1995 aged 89.

Carbury Close – Flight Lieutenant Brian Carbury DFC*

Born in Wellington, New Zealand on 27th February 1918, Brian John George Carbury was the son of a veterinary doctor. The family moved to Auckland and here, he was educated at New Lynn and Kings College. He was keen on sports and was a very good athlete, but also played cricket, rugby, tennis and swam, who became a member of the local water polo team. His other hobbies included playing the guitar and rifle shooting.

On leaving college in 1934, he joined Farmers Trading Company as a shoe salesman, but soon became bored with the job. He applied to join the Royal Navy in June 1937, when he travelled to Britain aged 19, but failed. But his next move to join the Royal Air Force was more successful and he was granted a short-service commission and started his flying training at No. 10 Elementary & Reserve Flying Training School at Yatesbury on 27th September 1937. Following completion of this course, he was posted to No. 41 Squadron at Catterick in June 1938, flying Hawker Fury biplanes.

Standing at six foot-four inches with dark wavy hair, he was probably one of the tallest in the Royal Air Force.

Towards the end of July, he joined the full-time contingent at RAF Brough, Yorkshire, as an instructor in a unit known as 'Harston's Flying Circus.' He returned to 41 Squadron in October 1938. In January 1939, the squadron was re-equipped with the new Supermarine Spitfire, but by October, Carbury was attached to 'A' Flight at Turnhouse up in Scotland to No. 603 Squadron to assist in conversion on the new aircraft. By 24th October, his temporary position with 603 became permanent.

His first success against the Germans came on 7th December, when whilst on patrol at around 12.30 pm accompanied by Flying Officer Laurie Cunningham and Sergeant Ras Berry, they sighted a formation of seven Heinkel bombers heading towards the airfield at Montrose. The Spitfires engaged the bombers and Carbury singled out one of the Heinkels to attack. He decided to engage the bomber with a frontal attack and fired short bursts before breaking away; observing white smoke pouring from the bomber's two engines. He returned to base claiming the enemy aircraft damaged.

Carbury was promoted in rank to flying officer on 27th April 1940. He was again able to share in the destruction of another enemy aircraft on 3rd July, when flying as part of Green Section they attacked a Junkers Ju88 at 9,000 feet off the coast of Montrose at 2.45 pm.

When the squadron moved to Hornchurch in late August, Carbury and the rest of his colleagues were thrown straight away into the battle and remarked about having to deal with so many enemy aircraft. 'You don't have to look for them; you have to look for a way out.' At the end of the first day of operations at Hornchurch, 603 had lost two pilots; Laurie Cunningham aged 23 and Don MacDonald 22 years. Carbury had been in action that day and was successful in badly damaging a Messerschmitt 109 over Dover. His report states:

I sighted the enemy aircraft (six Me109s). As they attacked leading sections, we kept in Vic formation, but broke as Me109s came down. I followed two through cloud, with three following. I fired a short two second burst at one Me109 from 300 yards closing to 200 yards, smoke emitted from the front of the cockpit and carried on at about 45 degrees dive for France, so I left him. I sighted another 109, gave him a full deflection burst, but lost him in cloud. I also lost the rest of the squadron, so returned to base.

Within the next following three days, Carbury shot down a further seven Messerschmitt Me109s showing his skill as an outstanding pilot and aerial marksman. One of his victims was Oberleutnant Hafer of I/JG26, whom he shot down near Hornchurch on 31st August. Hafer jumped from his doomed aircraft, but his body was found two days later in the Ingrebourne Creek with the parachute unopened. The aircraft crashed into the ground at Bridge Road, Rainham.

During the end of September, he would claim another six aircraft destroyed and on 24th September was notified that he was to be awarded a DFC for his achievements. The citation stated in the London Gazette reported the following:

During operations on the north east coast, Flying Officer Carbury led his section in an attack on two enemy aircraft. Both were destroyed. From 28th August 1940, to 2nd September 1940, he has, with his squadron, been continuously engaged against large enemy raids over Kent, and has destroyed eight enemy aircraft. Five of these were shot down during three successive engagements in one day.

Claiming further victories in October and receiving a further award on 25th October of a Bar to his DFC, by the end of the Battle of Britain, his tally stood at 15 aircraft enemy destroyed, 2 probables and 3 damaged.

The squadron remained operational in the south-east of England until mid-December and returned to Scotland, taking up position at Drem. It was here that Carbury claimed his last victory on Christmas Day 1940, when he damaged a Junkers Ju88 bomber near St. Abbs Head. On 30th December, he received notification of posting to take up the position of an instructor at 58 Operational Training Unit at Grangemouth; here he could pass on his valuable experience to the new pilots.

He was promoted in rank to flight lieutenant in April 1941 and remained with the unit when it became No. 2 Combat Training Wing.

Sometime in 1944, Carbury was dismissed under a dark cloud from the Royal Air Force in circumstances not fully known. Although married, this did not survive and a divorce was settled in 1948; he subsequently remarried and was living happily in Woburn near High Wycombe, when he was diagnosed with Leukaemia, dying soon after on 31st July 1961 aged 43. A memorial was erected to his memory in the town of his birth in Wellington, New Zealand.

Crawford-Compton Close - Air Vice-Marshal William Crawford-Compton DSO* DFC*

William Vernon Crawford-Compton was born on 2nd March 1915 in Invercargill, New Zealand, the son of William Gilbert Crawford-Compton who was a farm landowner. As a youngster, his main interest was the sea and yachting, but this later turned to flying.
He was educated at the New Plymouth High School.

In 1938, at the age of 22, he was a handsome, tall dark-haired athletic-looking individual with a great deal of charm and that same year was invited to become a crew member on the sailing ship named 'Lands End' an auxiliary-engine ketch, along with two other New Zealanders and a South African, who had planned to sail around the globe stopping at England along the way. Compton was determined that on reaching Britain he would apply to join the Royal Air Force.

The venture was unfortunately short lived as after only several days, the ship struck an uncharted reef off New Guinea and began to sink. They salvaged as much of the provisions they could muster and hastily built a life raft. They managed to sight land after a night on the makeshift raft and landed on Rousel Island. Here they managed to bargain with the natives who gave them a canoe to travel to the nearest white settlement and here they met a trader who got them passage aboard another ship bound for Samari, New Guinea, over 200-miles away. On arriving at Samari, Compton learned of a tramp-steamer named the 'Myrtlebank,' a four-thousand tonner, which would be sailing to Britain.

The captain was told of their misfortune and was sympathetic to their situation and took them on as crewmen; Compton was to work as a carpenter and his friend as an engineer. After nearly a year's passage stopping at ports such as Shanghai, Durban and Cape Town, the ship finally arrived at Liverpool on 6th September 1939, just three days after the beginning of the Second World War.

The following morning, Compton caught the train for London and on arrival headed straight for the RAF enlistment office. By the end of the day, he was Aircraftsman Compton AC2 RAF Number 905967. For the next six months he undertook the necessary routine of drill, sentry duty, peeling potatoes and washing dishes. He served as a steward in the Officers' Mess at RAF Duxford.

He applied for and was accepted for basic flying training and was sent to No. 57 Operational Training Unit. After qualifying as a pilot, his first posting was to No. 603 'City of Edinburgh' Squadron based at Drem in Scotland on 7th January 1941.

On 30th January, while returning from a practice flight, Compton misjudged his final approach and crashed on landing. Fortunately the aircraft was not too badly damaged, and he stepped out of the Spitfire unhurt. The squadron moved to RAF Turnhouse on 28th February and while here, Compton was admitted to Gogarburn Hospital on 7th March and was discharged on 12th. Two days later on 14th, he received news of his next posting; he was to pack his kit and travel down to RAF Driffield in Yorkshire to join the newly formed New Zealand fighter squadron No. 485. For the next six weeks, he and his fellow New Zealanders learned to fly as a unit, using old Spitfire Is and Mk IIs. By the 12th April 1941, the squadron had been granted operational status. One of Compton's fellow pilots, Harvey Sweetman recalls his time with the squadron during this period:

Bill was an action man, aggressive, but also a damn good pilot. I flew with him on quite a number of sorties, when the RAF was changing over from the defensive to the offensive against the Germans. Formations and tactics were evolving to suit the offensive requirements, and these conditions suited Bill's talents as a fighter pilot. As a member of the squadron, he joined in when we were off duty; one of his party tricks was to display the chest scars he had gained with the reef encounter during his trip to reach England. He would give a lurid blow by blow account of the incident.

Compton was promoted from sergeant pilot and granted a commission as a pilot officer on 23rd April 1941. On one mission over France, to act as top cover on 21st September, the squadron sighted a large number of enemy fighters five miles west of Douvres. Compton flying as Blue 3 in 'B' Flight recalled the following engagement:

I saw four Me109Fs dive on two Spitfires below and to one side of me. They pulled up in front of us about 250 to 300 yards away. I gave the fourth 109 a long burst of cannon and machine gun fire, following which his cockpit hood and a panel flew off. He dived then climbed vertically, stalled, went on his back, spun and dived away. I did not follow him down, as there were other enemy aircraft close by, but in my opinion the enemy aircraft was probably destroyed.

By the end of 1941, Crawford-Compton had shot down three enemy fighters, and by 1942 he had been promoted to flying officer. Claiming further victories against the enemy, he was awarded the DFC on 10th March 1942, the citation read:

This officer has participated in a large number of operational sorties. He has at all times displayed great dash and determination. He has destroyed 2 and probably destroyed another 2 enemy aircraft.

When the squadron was not on operations they would travel to London and visit the pubs and clubs. Jack Rae, a flight sergeant remembers one such occasion:

We visited one club named the Tartan Drive, a favourite downstairs bar hang-out for New Zealanders in London. That night, the boys became convinced that for some reason the most attractive girls seemed to swoon towards the Polish pilots, leaving nothing for us. Bill Compton suddenly stood up, said 'to hell with this,' and adopted a heavy Polish accent and immediately whisked off the most attractive female in the room. Long afterwards, he insisted that it had worked many times over. We often wondered what the woman thought of his shoulder flashes with the words 'New Zealand' emblazoned for the entire world to see. Perhaps they had their minds on other things other than reading.

He was made a flight commander and led the squadron on many operations over Northern France and Belgium operating from RAF Kenley. Towards the end of April, Compton had to make a forced-landing in his Spitfire as he came into land, when his aircraft's engine backfired and cut out. He landed heavily, short of the runway in a field and suffered a broken wrist with cuts and bruises. He was taken off operational flying for several weeks.

Following recovery from his accident Compton was posted from 485 to join 611 Squadron also based at Kenley on 22nd June. On 19th August, he was in the thick of the action once more during the combined services raid against Dieppe, flying five sorties that day and claiming one Me109 destroyed. His achievements were again recognised and he was awarded a Bar to his DFC during December 1942. On 27th December, Compton received notification that he was to become squadron commander of No. 64 Squadron based at RAF Hornchurch and on arrival found that the squadron was at Fairlop, Hornchurch's satellite airfield.

During his time at Hornchurch, Compton would lead the other squadrons that made up the 'Hornchurch Wing.' Their main missions during 1943, was to provide escorts for the British bombers and the American 8th Army Air Force, which was mainly raiding during daylight hours. When not providing cover for the bomber raids, they would try and attack targets of opportunity, German airfields, locomotives, enemy installations etc. Compton was promoted to Wing Commander Flying on 21st July 1943 and was awarded the American Silver Star medal having flown over 200 escort missions with the Americans. The award of the Distinguished Service Order was bestowed on him on 24th September 1943 stated:

Since being awarded the DFC, this officer has participated in a large number of sorties over enemy territory. By his masterly leadership, exceptional skills and gallant example, he has imbued the squadrons he commands with real zest for battle, combined with a high standard of operational efficiency. Wing Commander Crawford-Compton, who has destroyed at least 13 hostile aircraft and damaged several others, has rendered most valuable service.

That October, Compton along with Wing Commander Ray Harries DSO, DFC, who was commanding the Tangmere Wing, was sent to the United States on a tour to lecture on tactics. Here they gave talks to various audiences including universities and rotary clubs. Compton was interviewed thirteen times on radio. They returned to Britain in April 1944. At the end of that month, he was given the post of wing leader of No. 145 'Cross of Lorraine' Wing at Merston aerodrome. In overall command of the Wing was 'Sailor' Malan. This Wing was an all-French affair with 329, 340 and 341 Squadrons equipped with Spitfire Mk IXBs.

On the morning of the 6th June 1944, the Allies landed at Normandy on D-Day. The very next day Compton shot down his first and only German bomber, just inside the French coast and west of Caen. His final claim of the war came on 9th July 1944, when he destroyed a Messerschmitt 109, five miles north of Bernay. His outstanding achievement in air combat was notable, and his final tally of enemy aircraft destroyed was recorded as 20 and 1 shared destroyed, 3 and 1 shared probable and 13 damaged.

By wars end in Europe in May 1945, Compton had flown 800 hours operationally in Spitfires, a new record for Fighter Command.

His wishes to remain within the service were granted and on 1st September 1945, he was granted a permanent commission with the rank of squadron leader. He then undertook a six-month Staff College course at Haifa and on completion was sent to Air Command Staff Headquarters in the Middle East, stationed at Cairo. He remained there until 1947, when on return to Britain he joined the Air Ministry for policy duties.

During this time he met and married Chloe Clifford-Brown in 1949. He became Air Attaché in Oslo, Norway in 1950. He was awarded the Legion de Honour and Croix de Guerre with Palme.

In January 1955, he was promoted to group captain and given command of RAF Station Bruggen, Germany. During the Suez Crisis in Egypt, he was appointed commander of the Western Fighter Sector and was in charge of No. 215 Wing based at El Gamil airfield, Port Said, following the sea-borne landings by British forces.

Back in Britain in January 1957, Compton was appointed chief instructor at the School of Land-Air Warfare at Old Sarum in Wiltshire and on the 13th June was awarded the Commander of the Order of the British Empire (CBE) by Her Majesty the Queen at Buckingham Palace. He attained the rank of air commodore on 1st July 1960, and was on the staff of the Imperial Defence College in 1961. He was promoted to air vice-marshal on 1st July 1963 and made CB in the New Year's honours list in January 1965.

In 1967, he captained the Royal Air Forces Skiing Team, made up of men half his age. He finally retired after thirty-nine years of service on 1st November 1968. His first marriage ended in divorce in 1978 and he later remarried to Delores Pearl Goodhew, making him the stepfather of the British Olympic gold medal winner Duncan Goodhew.

William Crawford-Compton passed away suddenly on 2nd January 1988 aged 72 years, but the memory of this great New Zealand fighter pilot who worked his way through the RAF ranks and fought for England during its greatest need is remembered.

During the author's research of this book, the next named road was Dawson Drive. The author found that there were two possible pilots who could have been recommended by those who had put the names forward originally to have roads or streets named after them, as no records now exist within the London Borough of Havering. The author has included the two pilots below.

Dawson Drive – Sub-Lieutenant Francis Dawson-Paul

Francis Dawson-Paul was born on 18th February 1916. The author could not find any information regarding his early years other than he joined the Reserve of Air Force Officers (RAFO) and was commissioned in August 1934, but resigned due to ill-health. He joined the Royal Navy and transferred to the Fleet Air Arm for training on 26th September 1939 with 758 Squadron at HMS Raven at Eastleigh, Hampshire. After completion of a fighter aircraft course he was posted on loan to the Royal Air Force in May 1940, and sent to No.7 Operational Training Unit at Hawarden to convert on to Spitfires, from here he was sent to No. 64 Squadron.

Flying patrols with the squadron from Kenley, he claimed a quarter share in shooting down a Dornier 17 bomber on 1st July 1940, he then individually destroyed an Me109 two miles east of Rouen and damaged another near Hawkinge on 5th, but during the course of this action his aircraft was damaged and he had to force-land his Spitfire on return to base. During the next following weeks in July, he claimed a total of 7 and 1 shared destroyed, 1 unconfirmed destroyed and 1 damaged. His final claim came on 25th July 1940 over the Channel, when he was seen to engage a Messerschmitt 109, before he in turn was shot down into the sea. Having baled-out, Dawson-Paul was rescued by a German E-boat, but was severely wounded; he died of his wounds five days later. He is buried at Hardinghen churchyard in France.

Wing Commander H.L. Dawson DFC

Born on 19th February 1914, at Ellersilie, Auckland, New Zealand. Dawson joined the Royal Air Force after being granted a short service commission in 1934 and proceeded to rise through the ranks of the service. By 1941, he had risen to the rank of wing commander and on 4th December 1941 was posted as a wing commander flying at Hornchurch, his stay was only brief, but during the month he was there, he led No 64 and 411 (Canadian) Squadrons in sweeps over France. He was posted away from Hornchurch on 16th January 1942. Later he was posted to the besieged island of Malta, where he commanded the airfield at Hal Far during the second part of 1942. Here, he organised his squadrons ready to scramble, when German and Italian aircraft were picked up heading to attack the island and the airfields. He was already an experienced fighter pilot, who had already led Hurricanes on sweeps over France previously and had also made low-level reconnaissance flights over enemy held territory from Malta.

The author was unable to obtain any further information regarding H.L. Dawson's life or RAF career, but perhaps someone in the general public might be able help with further information in the future.

Deere Avenue – Air Commodore Alan Deere OBE, DSO, DFC*

The name and exploits of New Zealand fighter pilot Alan Deere became legendary with his RAF colleagues during the Second World War and to a wider audience in the late 1950s, with the release of his autobiography 'Nine Lives' and much more recent biography by this author 'Al Deere-wartime fighter pilot, peacetime commander.' He was a shy and modest man who regarded himself as nothing out of the ordinary and always maintained that as a fighter pilot, he had been doing the job for which he had been so effectively trained.

Alan Christopher Deere was born on 12th December 1917 in the small town of Westport, in the South Island of New Zealand. His father was Terence Joseph Deere, who worked for the railways and his mother, Theresa Curtain who worked in one of the town's stores when they first met. Alan was the third of six boys. His first fascination with aeroplanes came one day whilst he was playing marbles with

his young friends. They were suddenly distracted by an unfamiliar sound in the air, looking up they saw the shape of a biplane flying overhead. The aircraft was heading for the beach at Westport. The boys stopped their game and immediately ran in the direction that the biplane was heading. When they arrived on the beach, a large crowd of people had already gathered around the silver machine. He and his friends spent the next couple of hours marvelling at the biplane and he was lucky to get close enough for one of the adults to hoist him up to get a quick look into the cockpit. He remarked in later years:

As a boy I always wanted to fly, but in New Zealand at that time there was very little opportunity to do so before the last war. Aviation had barely made an impact in my country.

Deere was educated at the St. Canice's School from 1923, but following the family moving to Wanganui in 1930, he continued his education with the Roman Catholic Marist Brothers until he went to the Wanganui Technical College from 1931 to 1934.

At the college he did well both academically and physically. He excelled at sports and represented the college in cricket, rugby and boxing, and for the latter he also represented the town in the New Zealand Boxing Championships.

In 1934, Deere's interest in aviation was brought to the fore, when Wanganui's airport became host to the arrival of one of the aviation pioneers, Sir Charles Kingsford-Smith, who arrived in his aircraft, 'Southern Cross.' During his visit, he offered passenger flights at ten shillings per head.

This was an opportunity that the young Deere could not pass up and he managed to acquire the money for a flight from the money he had saved for doing odd jobs. During the flight he felt exhilarated and from that day on, he was hooked on the idea of somehow learning to fly and become a pilot.

After obtaining his qualifications, he left school and spent a year working as a sheep hand on a local farm, but found more substantial employment in 1935 as a clerk with Treadwell and Haggitt, a solicitors firm.

In 1936, after learning that the Royal Air Force was now recruiting pilots in the Dominion countries, his aspirations to learn to fly were reawakened. Deere applied after getting his parents to sign the recruitment papers and after appearing before a selection board and a medical was one of twenty-four men selected in New Zealand. He bid farewell to his family and began his journey to Britain aboard the passenger steamship 'Rangitane' on 23rd September 1937. After nearly five weeks at sea, the ship finally berthed at Tilbury Docks. From there, the New Zealand recruits boarded the train for London and arrived at New Zealand House, where they were greeted by Bill Jordon, the High Commissioner. After spending a few days of leisure, visiting the historic landmarks including a visit to the Tower of London, they were then sent to start their training.

On 25th October 1937, Deere began his flying training at De Havilland's No. 12 Elementary & Reserve Flying Training School at White Waltham. The following month, he went solo and by December had amassed 25-hours in his log-book. Deere was granted a short service commission on 9th January 1938 and by May that year had received the coveted RAF wings to display on his tunic. On 10th August 1938, Deere's training days had come to an end, he now awaited news of which squadron he would be posted. Within days, he received notification that his new posting was to be to No.54 Squadron based at RAF Hornchurch situated on the outskirts of East London.

On 20th August, Alan Deere and Arthur Charrett, a Canadian arrived by District Line train at Elm Park Underground station to take up their new posts at Hornchurch as acting pilot officers. His new squadron was equipped at this time with the Gloster Gladiator biplane, which was a joy to fly, but would soon become obsolete when the RAF brought into service the Hawker Hurricane and Supermarine Spitfire.

During the last two years before war was declared against Germany, Deere continued his sporting achievements by playing for the South London rugby team Rosslyn Park, playing in the position of inside centre on numerous occasions.

In March 1939, 54 Squadron received their first Spitfire aircraft and exchanged their old Gladiators with 603 Squadron based at Turnhouse in Scotland. Deere and the rest of his colleagues spent many hours getting to know the Spitfire's capabilities as a fighting machine, undertaking fighter formation and practice dogfights.

When war with Germany was declared on 3rd September 1939, the squadrons at Hornchurch were put on immediate alert, but it would be many months before they would see any action. It was not until May 1940, when after the Germans had launched their Blitzkrieg attack through France and Belgium and pushed the Allies back towards the port town of Dunkirk, that Deere would see his first action of the war.

On 23rd May, with the Royal Navy tasked with evacuating the retreating British army off the beaches at Dunkirk, the RAF were tasked with providing air cover over that area to protect the troops from aerial attack by the German Luftwaffe, as they waited embarkation. 54 Squadron patrolled between Calais and Dunkirk during the morning patrol, but this was uneventful. On return to Hornchurch, they learned that the commander of 74 Squadron, also based at Hornchurch; had been shot down, but had successfully landed his aircraft at Calais-Marck airfield.

It was decided that a rescue attempt of Squadron Leader White could be undertook by flying a two-seat Miles Master aircraft supported by an escort of two Spitfires. Flying the Master would be Flight Lieutenant James Leathart and his escort would be Alan Deere and Johnny Allen, all members of 54 Squadron.

The three aircraft took off and flew low across the Channel. On arrival at Calais-Marck, Leathart landed the Miles Master, while Deere and Allen climbed to various altitudes to cover the rescue in case enemy aircraft were in the vicinity. Leathart could find no sign of Squadron Leader White and prepared to take-off again. Suddenly, his aircraft was attacked by Messerschmitt 109 fighters and he was forced to land and scramble to the nearest ditch, here he expectantly found the squadron leader. Alan Deere immediately went into action and fired upon one of the German fighters and shot it down before engaging another and claiming it as damaged. Johnny Allen in the meantime had his hands full when he was attacked by five Me109s, but managed to survive and claim one destroyed, before quickly heading back home across the Channel.

Once the action had finished both Leathart and White jumped back into the Miles Master, just as German tanks began to advance up the road near the airfield and headed for home, landing at Manston to refuel before arriving back at Hornchurch at lunchtime. It was years later that it was recorded that Al Deere was the first Spitfire pilot to have combat with a Messerschmitt 109.

Deere continued to fly operations over Dunkirk, but on 28th May, he was to be on the receiving end, when he was shot down by the rear-gunner of a Dornier 17 bomber, he was about to attack. The bullets punctured his Spitfires radiator and he was forced to crash-land his aircraft on a beach between Nieuport and Ostend. On landing, Deere was knocked out momentarily when his head hit the gun-site, causing a gash on his forehead. Luckily, he managed to get first-aid from women at a nearby café and then found transport to take him to Dunkirk, where after a long wait; he managed to get aboard a destroyer and back to Dover.

On 14th June 1940, he was recognised for his bravery in combat with the award of a DFC. The recommendation stated in the London Gazette:

During the period of 21st to 28th May 1940 inclusive, Pilot Officer Deere has, in company of his squadron taken part in a large number of offensive patrols over Northern France, and has been engaged in seven combats, in some of which his squadron was outnumbered by as many as six to one.

In the course of these combats he shot down two Me110s, two Me109s and one Ju88 himself, and one Me109 and one Ju88 in conjunction with other members of his section, all of which are confirmed. Throughout these engagements this officer has shown great courage and determination in pressing home his attacks in the face of great odds, and his skill and offensive spirit has enabled him to destroy or damage seven enemy aircraft.

Seven days later, on 27 June at RAF Hornchurch, Deere, Leathart and Allen of 54 Squadron with Malan of 74 Squadron and Tuck of 92 Squadron were awarded medals by King George VI. Deere would later recall it was one of the greatest moments of his life.

With the fall of France, Britain now stood alone against Nazi Germany and waited for Herr Hitler's next move. Undoubtedly, an invasion would be put into operation, but when and where? The Royal

Air Force still patrolled the English Channel and a few interceptions were made against German reconnaissance aircraft.

At the beginning of July, RAF fighters were mainly doing convoy patrols, and engaging German dive-bombers and their escort fighters as they attacked shipping bringing vital supplies into British ports.

During the late afternoon of 9th July, Al Deere was leading Red Section between Deal and Dover, when they became involved in an action against the enemy and Deere had a close brush with death. His report of the combat stated:

I was leading 'A' Flight on a patrol over Deal at 6,000 feet when I sighted a silver seaplane approaching Deal at 100 feet. Four Me109s were flying above in front. I ordered Yellow Leader (Johnny Allen) to attack the seaplane with his section. I led my section towards the 109s, but on doing so, saw about another 12 109s flying in loose formation close to the water.

I ordered my section into line astern, but apparently the order was not received as the pilots broke away to engage the enemy. I attacked the tail-end aircraft of the original four from above and behind. It dived straight into the sea after I had fired two bursts into it. I then pulled up, climbing for height and reported to home station that the seaplane had landed in the water, ten miles east of deal.

I then dived down to attack the seaplane, but saw an Me109 endeavouring to position itself on my tail. I turned towards him and opened fire at about 1,000 yards head-on. He was also firing and I could hear bullets striking my fuselage. We both held our fire and apparently my propeller hit some of his fuselage as he passed close overhead, because two tips were bent right back and my canopy hood had been pushed in. The engine vibrated tremendously and then stopped, smoke then began to billow out. I was heading landwards at the time of collision and carried on for an open field. Flames then appeared at 1,000 feet and I was unable to see ahead, I eventually crash-landed in a field. The aircraft was burning fiercely, but I managed to break the hood open and get out with slight injury.

Deere had crash-landed his Spitfire at Gunstan Farm, Ash, five miles from Manston.

From 10th July till 31st October, the official dates of the Battle of Britain, Deere and 54 Squadron were heavily involved in combats day after day against the might of the German Luftwaffe and suffered many casualties. On numerous times Deere escaped death both in the air and on the ground. On 15th August, he was shot down by a Me109 and just managed to vacate his Spitfire, when his parachute became caught within the cockpit. He broke free, but struck his right wrist a glancing blow on the tail plane. He landed amongst some tall trees; his only injury was a sprained wrist. He was shot down again on 28th August 1940. Deere believed this time he was a victim of friendly fire.

When at 23,000 feet, I was shot down by a Spitfire (no markings observed). My control wires to the rudder were shot away and I had to bale-out.

He came down near Detling and suffered slight injuries when he landed astride a small plumb tree in an orchard. He was checking himself over, when he was confronted by an angry and red-faced farmer brandishing a shot-gun, shouting 'why did you have to land on my prize plum tree?'

On 31st August, Deere escaped perhaps the most harrowing of his experiences, when his squadron were caught on the ground at Hornchurch, when an unseen enemy formation raided the aerodrome. As the first bombs began to explode, 54 Squadron hastily prepared to take-off. The first section led by James Leathart managed to get airborne, but the following three Spitfires which included Al Deere was caught as they tried to take-off. A bomb exploded near to his aircraft tossing the Spitfire on to its back, careering it along the ground for 100 yards, before it came to a halt. Pilot Officer Edsall's aircraft had a wing torn off, but stayed the right way up; while Sergeant Davis was blown over the Ingrebourne Creek which ran alongside the aerodrome. Eric Edsall was unhurt and scrambled from his aircraft and ran over to Deere's Spitfire.

Deere was trapped inside his aircraft which was now leaking fuel. Edsall managed to pry open the cockpit side door and drag out the concussed Deere. He helped him to the nearest first-aid post, where Deere was given medical help, having suffered having part of his scalp torn away and cuts and bruises. Sergeant Davis turned up an hour later with his parachute under his arm, having walked around the perimeter of the aerodrome to get back in. Deere was bandaged up and told to rest for 24-hours, but he was flying again the next day. It was a miracle that all three pilots had survived.

On 3rd September Deere and the remaining pilots were ordered up to Catterick in Yorkshire for a rest period, and three days later he learnt he had been awarded a second DFC. The squadron spent the remainder of 1940 at Catterick, Deere spending most of his time air-testing new Spitfires or giving new pilots practice flights and passing on his combat experience. It was here that on 28th December, he took off with Sergeant Howard Squire on a dogfight practice.

At 10,000 feet Deere ordered Squire to try and latch on to his aircraft as he would take evasive action as in a real combat. After a couple of encounters Deere could not see Squire's Spitfire, but in an instant there was an almighty bang, as Deere's Spitfire was cut in two, the tail-plane falling away and his Spitfire whipped into a vicious spin, completely out of control. Deere baled-out only to find the handle of his ripcord had been torn away and was out of reach. Then as the ground became uncomfortably close, miraculously the parachute opened of its own accord and the next second he landed in a thick, foul stinking farmyard cesspool.

Deere was in agony and could hardly move. A passing motorist and his wife came to his aid, and drove him seven miles to Catterick Hospital. After an X-Ray, it was revealed he had a chipped coccyx at the base of the spine. He was not hospitalised, but told to rest in bed for several days.

Sergeant Squire had also baled-out of his Spitfire, which had caught fire on impact with Deere's aircraft, but he landed uninjured.

On recovery from his lucky escape, Deere was given the non-flying job as a operations controller at Catterick and it was during this period that he would meet his future wife Joan Fenton, who served as a driver in the American Ambulance, Great Britain.

Deere was itching to get back flying operationally and his wish was granted on 6th May 1941, when he was given the post of flight commander with No. 602 'City of Glasgow' Squadron based at Ayr on the east coast of Scotland. On 10th July 1941, the squadron received its marching orders and was sent south to operate from RAF Kenley; here they would undertake offensive operations over Europe in operations escorting bombers or 'Rhubarbs' offensive sweeps made up of fighter formations only. Between 1st August and 18th November, Deere would claim one Me109 destroyed and four damaged.

Towards the end of February 1942, he was taken off operations and was asked to visit America as part of an RAF Delegation to Washington DC, where he would give talks about his combat experiences. He arrived in Washington on 4th March 1942, but after six weeks of touring and lectures, he began to tire of this type of work and felt he would serve better if he was sent back to Britain to return to operational flying. His wishes were granted and he returned to Britain to take command of No. 403 (Canadian) Squadron at North Weald on 25th April. Here he led the squadron up until 13th August, when he was posted to Headquarters No.13 Group, but this was only a short stay before he was again posted to attend an officers' staff training course at the RAF Staff College at Gerrards Cross in Buckinghamshire on 26th October, on completion he was again moved back to Headquarters 13 Group and it was not until 11th February 1943 that he was sent to fly operationally as a supernumerary squadron leader flying to RAF Biggin Hill, commanded by his old Hornchurch friend 'Sailor' Malan.

Here Deere was given leadership of a section of the Biggin Hill Wing and became its new wing leader on 14th March. Here he flew many operations during the next six months, notching up an impressive score against the enemy, claiming 3 Focke-Wulf 190s destroyed, 1 probable and 1 damaged. On 4th June 1943, he was awarded the Distinguished Service Order.

Towards the end of September, the aerodrome was suddenly struck down with a severe outbreak of dysentery, which affected a lot of the pilots; one of them was Al Deere. After recovering, it was decided that he should come off operational flying and given a rest period. As soon as he was fit again, he was given the job as Chief Instructor of the Fighter Wing at the Central Gunnery School at Sutton Bridge on 21st October 1943. He remained at this post until 20th March 1944 before posted to No. 11 Group Headquarters as a member of the air staff, the commander being no less than his old station commander at Hornchurch, Cecil Bouchier.

In April 1944, while working at 11 Group, he received the amazing news that he was again to become operational. Bouchier told him that the Air Officer commanding 84 Group had contacted him with regard to Deere taking command of the Free French fighter squadrons in his group. After being released from his duties, Deere arrived on 1st May at Merston airfield near Chichester, Sussex to take command of 145 Wing, which was part of 2nd Tactical Air Force. At the beginning of June, they moved to the advanced airfield at Selsey in preparation for the Normandy Invasion. Deere travelled up to RAF Uxbridge with two-hundred other senior officers and sat in the station cinema to await details of 'Operation Overlord.' Deere later recalled that momentous day of 6th June 1944-D-Day.

I had two French squadrons under me; they made a special request, so I was sent down to lead their wing up to and including D-Day. I can remember the expressions on the faces of those gallant Frenchmen when I briefed them about the invasion. Many had tears running down their faces, full of hope and joy. On D-Day the weather was particularly bad and we didn't see very much along the beachhead; we actually went over as cover, just north of Caen. It was a marvellous sight to see all those ships below.

Soon after, Deere was taken off operations on 21st July and posted to the Headquarters of 84 Group, Control Centre in his new role as Wing Commander Plans. The job entailed moving forward with a mobile unit when the army advanced and co-ordinating air to ground strikes against the Germans. He continued in this role until the Germans finally surrendered in May 1945.

On 18th September, he married his fiancée Joan at St. Pancras Register Office in London and in December was given command of RAF Duxford in Cambridgeshire and was awarded the OBE on 1st June 1946. For the next twenty years, he was given other appointments including Assistant Commandant at RAF Cranwell and Commander of HQ 12 (East Anglian) Sector, his final post was as commandant of No.1 School of Technical Training, RAF Halton in January 1966. He finally retired from the Royal Air Force on 12th December 1967 with the rank of air commodore.

Alan Deere died on 21st September 1995 after a long battle with cancer. He is not only remembered by the road named after him, but also having one of the school houses at the R.J. Mitchell School bearing his name.

Denholme Walk – Group Captain George Lovell Denholm DFC

(Please note street sign is misspelt)

George Denholm was born at Bo'ness, West Lothian, Scotland on 20th December 1908, the third son of William and Minnie Denholm (nee Lovell) at the family home 'Tidings Hill, Cadow Crescent. He was educated at Cargilfield Prep School and Fettes School before attending St John's College at Cambridge. Here he studied economics and law and also joined the University Cadet Corps where he learnt how to ride and worked with horses pulling gun carriages. Following his graduation from Cambridge, he returned to the family business of coal-exporters, but was disinterested in this role. He became interested in flying and joined the Edinburgh Flying Club at Macmerry and East Fortune in East Lothian in the early 1930s to take private flying lessons.

In June 1933, he applied to join No. 603 Auxiliary Air Force Squadron and was accepted and attained a commission as a pilot officer on 27th June that year. By December 1934, he had been promoted to flying officer and in 1937 was qualified as a flying instructor. In January 1939, he had reached the rank of flight lieutenant. Although flying was his main concern, he did enjoy other activities such as riding, tennis, sailing golf and skiing.

With the outbreak of war against Germany looking imminent Denholm and the rest of his squadron were called to full-time service on 23rd August 1939 and was by this time an experienced flight commander at the age of 31 years. Because he was considerably older than many of the younger men in the squadron, he was given the nickname of 'Uncle' George.

Denholm married Betty Toombs on 29th November 1939 in Linlithgow with the pipe band of 603 Squadron playing as they entered the church.

His first action against the enemy took place on 16th October 1939, when 603 attacked a German Heinkel bomber over the Firth of Forth.

He claimed a share in its destruction; the first enemy aircraft of the war to be brought down on British soil. He had further success in March 1940, when he damaged a Dornier 17 off Petershead near Aberdeen at 9.15 am. On 5th June 1940, Denholm was appointed acting squadron leader of 603 Squadron taking over from Squadron Leader Stevens who had medical problems. Claims continued with the probable destruction of a Heinkel 111 on 26th and a shared victory over a Junkers Ju88 on 3rd July.

As the intensity of the Battle of Britain heightened during July and August, 603 Squadron were finally called south to Hornchurch and led by George Denholm arrived on Tuesday 27th August 1940. They were thrown into action the very next day, their first patrol taking off at 12.27 pm to intercept a formation of enemy aircraft over Kent. Denholm relates the interception in his combat report:

When 20-miles west of Canterbury we saw 12 Me109s in vics of three at 22,000 feet. I was at the same height and got on to the tail of a Me109, followed it through cloud and fired at range of 80 yards with a two second burst, firing 240-rounds. The enemy aircraft went into a vertical dive with a long vapour trail, which I thought was glycol fumes. After that I did not see the enemy aircraft again.

Denholm was again in action later that day leading a patrol of 11 Spitfires at 6.36 pm; at 7.36 pm 10-miles west of Manston he sighted 10 Me109s. He led his men down to attack the German aircraft, diving with the sun behind them. His report of the combat read:

I singled out a Me109 and made two stern attacks at it, and after the second attack, it appeared to be in difficulties. I was then able to make two quarter attacks and the pilot, who had been heading for France, turned back towards the coast and glided down to land. I saw him hit high-tension wires and crash into a field west of Dover.

Fortunately, the pilot Otto Schottle managed to get himself clear of his burning aircraft, suffering from a head wound and gave himself up. Denholm claimed one probable and one destroyed that day. Two days later on Friday 30th August, this time he would be on the receiving end, when leading six Spitfires against a formation of 80 Messerschmitt 110s which had formed into defensive circles and various heights, his Spitfire was badly damaged by enemy fire and he was forced to bale-out over Deal. His aircraft crashing to earth at Hope Farm, Snargate; fortunately he landed unhurt accept for some bruises.

On 1st September, he damaged a further Me109 and on 15th claimed two Dornier 17s damaged and another 109 destroyed, but later that day was again shot down and had to take to his parachute; he landed near Guestling Lodge, Kent.

Over the next month and a half, he claimed many more enemy aircraft destroyed or damaged and by the end of October 1940, his score stood at 3 and 3 shared destroyed, 1 unconfirmed destroyed 3 and 1 probables, 6 damaged.

He was awarded the Distinguished Flying Cross on 22nd October 1940, his citation read:

Since the commencement of hostilities, Squadron Leader Denholm has led his squadron, flight or section in innumerable operational patrols against the enemy. His magnificent leadership has contributed largely to the success of the squadron, which has destroyed fifty-four enemy aircraft in about six weeks; four of these aircraft destroyed by Squadron Leader Denholm himself.

No. 603 'City of Edinburgh' Squadron remained at RAF Hornchurch until 17th December 1940 and then returned to Scotland at RAF Drem. Denholm relinquished his command of the squadron in April 1941 and was posted to become a controller in the operations room at RAF Turnhouse. He was given command of a new unit, 1460 Flight which was forming at Acklington on 15th December 1941, with Turbainlite-Havocs.

He remained with them until March 1942, until he was given command of No. 605 Squadron at RAF Ford, Sussex in August. His final victory over an enemy aircraft came on 11th March 1943, when on a night-intruder operation flying Mosquito aircraft over Gilze-Rijen, Netherlands, he shot down an unidentified enemy aircraft. He was posted away from 605 Squadron in May 1943. At the end of hostilities in 1945, he was demobbed with the rank of acting group captain and returned to take up the family business of J&J Denholm until retirement in 1980, but remained active with attending 603 Squadron re-unions. He died in 15th June 1997.

Dewey Path – Pilot Officer Robert Basil Dewey

Robert Basil Dewey was born in Barnet, North London in June 1921, to Allan and Violet Dewey and joined the Royal Air Force on a short service commission in August 1939. After completing his flying training he was sent on 18th May 1940 to No.5 Operational Training Unit at Aston Down to convert on to Spitfire aircraft and on completion of the course was posted to No. 611 Squadron at RAF Digby on 26th June.

He joined No. 603 Squadron based at Hornchurch on 27th September 1940 and three days later claimed his first enemy aircraft, a Messerschmitt 109. It was not until October 20th that he claimed another, again a 109 fighter. On 27th October, Dewey was shot down during a surprise attack by Me109s of JG/51 south of Maidstone. His Spitfire was badly damaged and on trying to crash-land, he hit a tree at Apple Tree Corner, Chartham Hatch at 2.05 pm and was killed. His body was returned to Hornchurch and he now lies buried at St. Andrew's Church cemetery in the military plot.

Dowding Way – Wing Commander Derek Dowding AFC

Derek Hugh Tremenheere Dowding was born on 9th January 1919, the son of Hugh and Clarice Dowding who lived at Moseley, Carr-Lane, Acomb, North Yorkshire. His father, a group captain at the time, would rise in rank to become Air Chief Marshal Sir Hugh Dowding Commander-in- Chief of Fighter Command during the Battle of Britain. He was educated at Winchester College and then went to the RAF College at Cranwell, Lincolnshire as a flight cadet in September 1937. Following his graduation, he was commissioned as a pilot officer on 29th July 1939 and posted to No. 74 Squadron at RAF Hornchurch.

It was not until May 1940 that he would see action, patrolling over France from 20th May, when 74 Squadron was tasked in protecting the Dunkirk evacuation. On 23rd May, he shared in shooting down a Junkers Ju88 bomber and the following day claimed a share in Dornier 17 and probably destroyed another Ju88. Again on 27th May he damaged a Dornier after a chase of 20 miles before he had to disengage due to the amount of anti-aircraft fire he encountered.

Dowding probably destroyed a Heinkel 111 on 6th July and damaged another on the 8th July, but his time with 74 Squadron ended when he was posted to No. 6 Operational Training Unit at Sutton Bridge to become an instructor on 8th August 1940. He was to remain here and was promoted to the rank of flight lieutenant when posted to 135 Squadron later that year. Between 1942 and 1945, he was involved in test piloting aircraft in the Middle East.

After the war, he continued to serve in the RAF, including commander of RAF Upwood before retiring as a wing commander on 17th November 1956. He died on 22 November 1992 aged 73.

Edridge Close – Flying Officer Hilary Edridge

Hilary Patrick Mary Edridge was born 20th January 1919 and was the son of Doctor Raymond Edridge, a skin specialist of 29 Gay Street, Bath, Somerset. The name of Mary within his name was quite a common thing in devoutly Roman Catholic families, which the Edridge's were. Many boys born into the Roman Catholic faith had the name of Mary, as one of their names, but never the first name, of course!

He was educated at Stonyhurst College and was commissioned in the 4th Battalion, Somerset Light Infantry before he joined the Royal Air Force on a short service commission in January 1939 and was sent to No. 13 Elementary and Reserve Flying Training School at White Waltham and qualified as a pilot on 21st February 1939. Edridge then went to 13 Flying Training School and RAF Drem, East Lothian, Scotland and on 21st October that year was a pilot officer.

He was posted to No. 222 Squadron based at RAF Duxford in April 1940, at that time they were converting from Bristol Blenheims to Spitfire aircraft. The squadron moved then to Kirton-in-Lindsey, Lincolnshire. During the end of May, they were called south to Hornchurch to take part in operations over the French coast during the Dunkirk evacuation and on 1st June, Edridge claimed a Me109 probably destroyed. His combat report of the action read:

Enemy fighters sighted in line astern. I saw three dive to sea level pursued by a few of our fighters; the remainder circled and engaged us. I saw a Me109 dive past me evidently having fired at me from behind though I noticed no tracer or cannon shell. I eventually got fairly easily on his tail and got in a long burst. Immediately he slowed down, I presumed his engine had stopped and white smoke and flames appeared, I could not confirm this as I had to break away with a Me110 on my tail-firing inaccurately with tracer. No hits to my machine. About half my ammunition was expended.

Once the evacuation had ended, the squadron moved back to Kirton until recalled south once more for the Battle of Britain on 29th August 1940. The next day, the squadron was attacked during a patrol from Rochford at 5.10 pm by enemy fighters and during this action Edridge's Spitfire K9826 was hit and he was forced to bale-out. He landed suffering from burns to his face at Broome Park; his aircraft crashing at Marley near Barham.

He was flying on 15th October, when his Spitfire suffered engine failure and he was obliged to make a forced-landing at Tillingham Hall, near Horndon, he landed without injury to himself. His next victory came on 20th October, when he was able to claim a share in destroying a Messerschmitt 110 fighter-bomber near Maidstone.

Tragically, Hilary Edridge was shot down again on 30th October, when he came under attack from a number of German fighters. Having received a wound to the head and his aircraft ablaze, he managed to steer the stricken Spitfire and avoid Great Dixter House, before crashing at Longwood Farm, Ewhurst in Sussex. His aircraft overturned on landing, but almost immediately, he was pulled free from the wreckage by locals and his wounds dressed. He was rushed to an emergency hospital at Brickwell House, Northiam, but sadly he never regained consciousness and died that day. He was buried in the Roman Catholic Cemetery, Perrymead, Widcombe, Bath. He was 21 years old.

Esmond Close–Lieutenant Commander Eugene Esmonde VC, DSO

Note sign is misspelt missing letter e

Eugene Kingsmill Esmonde was born in Thurgoland, Wortley near Barnsley, South Yorkshire on 1st March 1909, the son of Dr John Joseph Esmonde and his wife Eily, who at the time was in temporary general practice. His parents were of Irish blood and as a young boy frequently returned to the ancestral home in Drominagh, North Tipperary. He received his education taught by Jesuits at Wimbledon College in London and then in Ireland at Clongowes Wood College, County Kildare.

He joined the Royal Air Force becoming a pilot officer on probation on 28th December 1928 and was attached to the Fleet Air Arm, serving the remainder of his five year commission out in the Mediterranean. On finishing his time with the RAF, he obtained a job working with Imperial Airways in August 1934, serving as a First Officer. During his time with this company he flew on the mail routes from London to Glasgow and to the Middle East and India. In 1935, he survived a serious accident when his aircraft crashed at Irrawaddy. Esmonde was promoted to the rank of captain on 3rd July 1937 and was one of the first pilots to fly the new giant Sunderland flying boats, now taking mail from Britain to Australia.

In 1939, with war looming, he resigned from Imperial Airways and joined the Fleet Air Arm to take up a commission as a lieutenant commander. His first posting was aboard the aircraft carrier HMS Courageous. The ship was on anti-submarine patrol off the coast of Ireland on 17th September 1939, with an escort of four destroyers, when she was hit by two torpedoes on the port side. She capsized and sank within fifteen minutes with the loss of 518 men. Esmonde was one of the lucky survivors. The U-boat responsible was U-29 captained by Otto Schuhart. Courageous was the first British warship to be sunk in WW2.

Following his lucky escape, he was given shore duties, serving at the Royal Navy Air Station at Lee-on-Solent. In May 1941, Esmonde was posted to serve aboard HMS Victorious and was involved with the hunt for the German pocket-battleship Bismarck following the sinking of HMS Hood with the loss of all but three of her crew on 24th May 1941.

That night, Esmonde led nine Fairey Swordfish torpedo biplanes in an attack against the Bismarck. On finding the enemy vessel, they dived down to launch their torpedoes amidst a barrage of heavy anti-aircraft fire, but only scored one hit on the starboard side. This had hardly any effect on the German battleship, but an attack from another squadron launched from HMS Ark Royal managed to damage the Bismarck's rudder, leaving her unable to steer. The following day, she was overcome by superior British naval forces and sunk. For his actions during this action, Esmonde was awarded the Distinguished Service Order.

He was posted to command a squadron on the HMS Ark Royal and was aboard her when she was torpedoed on 14th November 1941 by U-boat U-81, while sailing in the western Mediterranean. Attempts to tow the carrier to Gibraltar were in vain and the crew were ordered to abandon ship. However, some of her crew were transported by the ship's Swordfish aircraft before she finally sank. Esmonde was Mentioned in Despatches for his actions that day. On arrival in England, Esmonde returned to Lee-on- Solent and remained there until the beginning of February 1942.

On 12th February, Esmonde and his squadron, No.825 were standing ready at RAF Manston, Kent. The airfield was situated on the coast of the English Channel. That day, news was received that three German warships had broken out of the French port of Brest trying to make for the German port of Wilhelmshaven. The German ships were the battle-cruisers Scharnhorst, the Gneisenau and heavy cruiser the Prinz Eugen escorted by destroyers with Luftwaffe fighter air-cover; Code-named 'Operation Cerberus' by the Germans. Alerted to the break-out, the RAF had sent reconnaissance aircraft to monitor the ships progress in the Channel, before launching an attack.

Esmonde and his squadron were given orders to attack the battleships, but to wait for fighter escort provided by three squadrons of Spitfire aircraft from 64, 72 and 411 Squadrons. Manston was being controlled by RAF Hornchurch's Operations Room during this time.

At 12.25 pm, with no sign of his fighter escort, Esmonde could wait no longer and decided to get his six aircraft airborne, although it would be suicidal to attack without air-cover. One of the fighter squadrons did finally arrive, but 15-minutes too late.

Arriving over the targets, the Swordfish were met with heavy enemy fire and above German fighters were everywhere. By the time they prepared to launch their attack Esmonde's aircraft had suffered severe damage; his port wing had been shot to ribbons. Having dropped his torpedo, his aircraft was again hit at a range of 3,000 yards and crashed into the sea, killing all three aboard. The five other remaining aircraft were also shot down during the attack, only five airmen of the eighteen survived. None of their torpedoes hit the ships.

Admiral Bertram Ramsey later wrote of the incident: 'In my opinion, the gallant sortie of these six Swordfish aircraft constitutes one of the finest exhibitions of self-sacrifice and devotion to duty, the war had ever witnessed.'

All three German ships eventually reached safety, although the Scharnhorst had been damaged by mines. The surviving Swordfish airmen were all given awards; four officers received the DSO and an air-gunner the Conspicuous Gallantry Medal.

Esmonde's body was washed ashore seven weeks later, still in his life-jacket near the River Medway. He was awarded a posthumous Victoria Cross on 3rd March 1942 and was buried with full military honours at Woodlands Cemetery, Gillingham, Kent. Esmonde's VC citation reads:

The King has been graciously pleased to approve the grant of the Victoria Cross, for valour and resolution in action against the enemy to: The late Lieutenant Commander Eugene Esmonde, DSO, Royal Navy:

On the morning of Thursday 12th February, 1942, Lieutenant Commander Esmonde, in command of a Squadron of Fleet Air Arm, was told that the German Battle-Cruisers Scharnhorst and Gneisenau and the Cruiser Prinz Eugen, strongly escorted by thirty surface craft, were entering the Straits of Dover, and that his squadron must attack before they reached the sand-banks north-east of Calais.

Lieutenant Commander Esmonde knew well that his enterprise was desperate. Soon after noon, he and his squadron of six Swordfish set course for the enemy, and after ten minutes flight were attacked by a strong force of enemy fighters.

He lost touch with his fighter escort; and in action which followed, all his aircraft were damaged. He flew on, cool and resolute, serenely challenging hopeless odds, to encounter the deadly fire of the battle-cruisers and their escort, which shattered the port wing of his aircraft.

Undismayed, he led the squadron on, straight through this inferno of fire, in steady flight towards the target. Almost at once he was shot down; but his squadron went on to launch a gallant attack, in which at least one torpedo is believed to have struck the German battle-cruiser, and from which not one of the six aircraft returned. His high courage and splendid resolution will live in the traditions of the Royal Navy, and remain for many generations a fine and stirring memory.

Finucane Gardens – Wing Commander Brendan 'Paddy' Finucane DSO, DFC*

Born in Dublin, Ireland on 16th October 1920, Brendan Eamonn Finucane was the first son of Thomas and Florence Finucane nee Robinson. He was educated at both the two Rathmines Primary Schools, one at Marlborough Street, the other at Synge Street. It was during this time that his father took him and his younger brother Raymond to an air display at Baldonnell in 1932, here the first seeds of aviation were sown within the young Brendan Finucane's mind following a ten-minute joyride flight.

His education continued at the Roman Catholic Christian Brothers O'Connell School, which also had a fine sporting tradition. Finucane was a keen sportsman and excelled at Rugby and became the captain of the first team. On leaving school he joined an accountancy firm, but his father who was now a company director, decided to move the whole family to Richmond, England. On arrival in London, he managed to get an office job in Regent Street, but after a few months was totally bored with this position. Seeing an advertisement that the Royal Air Force was expanding and offering short service commissions, he decided to apply and in June 1938, he went for an interview at the Air Ministry and was accepted. It was during this time that his nickname of 'Paddy' was adopted by his friends.

Two months later he was ordered to report to the flying training school at Sywell, Northants on 29th August. On completion of this, he was sent to No. 1 RAF Depot at Uxbridge in October and then up to Montrose, Scotland to No.8 Flying Training School on 12th November. He remained here for seven months before being posted to 13 Maintenance Unit at Henlow on 26th June 1939 in the Practice and Test Flight. He was here for almost a year before being sent to No.7 Operational Flying Unit at Hawarden on 28th June 1940 to convert on to Spitfire aircraft.

Finucane was then posted to No. 65 Squadron based at Hornchurch to arrive on the 15th July, but was so eager that he actually arrived on

13th. He joined 'B' Flight and for the next several days did a few practice flights before the squadron was moved down to operate from Rochford airfield near Southend.

His first patrol was quite eventful, when on 24th July, his Spitfire developed a glycol leak after being airborne for only ten minutes and his cockpit began to fill with choking white vapour. His radio also broke down and he had to force-land back at the airfield; his aircraft hitting a natural hollow in the airfields surface, causing damage to his undercarriage and he landed wheels up with a seized engine. Finucane fortunately walked away uninjured.

His first victory against the enemy came on 12th August 1940, the squadron had been scrambled and at 11.30 am at an altitude of 26,000 feet and ten miles out from the coast of North Foreland, they sighted twenty to thirty Messerschmitt 109s below them. They dived down to attack and Finucane managed to latch on to the tail of one of the enemy. Firing from a range of 250 yards, his victim began to pour grey smoke and dived into the Channel.

Landing at Manston airfield, the squadron barely had time to refuel, when the airfield came under a surprise attack from German aircraft. All of 65 Squadron's Spitfires managed to get airborne again except one, whose pilot dashed for the nearest slit trench. Coming out of cloud after the hairy take-off, Finucane attacked a Me109 over Margate and claimed it probably destroyed, having to break away quickly, he then ran across another which he fired at and claimed damaged. The following day he was again successful, shooting down two more German aircraft.

At the end of August 1940, Finucane and 65 Squadron were rested and sent up to Turnhouse in Scotland. He was promoted to flying officer on 3rd September and the squadron commander Laurence Holland's report of him read:

I have great hopes of this officer. He is keen and intelligent and shows likelihood of becoming a very efficient leader. Is being trained as a leader and is learning quickly.

On November 29th 1940, the squadron moved south again and were sent to RAF Tangmere in West Sussex. There was little enemy activity during the daylight hours during the following winter months, but on 4th January 1941, Finucane whilst leading a section of the squadron during a mid-morning patrol at 9.50 am came across a lone Messerschmitt 110 flying off Selsey Bill at 4,000 feet. Sighting the RAF aircraft, the German turned tail and headed back to France; and after four attacks by the Spitfires in a 15-minute chase, Finucane finally finished the German aircraft with two attacks from astern, sending it into the Channel. His tally of aircraft continued, destroying a Junkers Ju 88 bomber on 19th January, five miles off Cherbourg and an Me109 on 5th February ten miles off Cap D' Alprech.

His last claim with 65 Squadron came on 15th April during a Wing sweep over Boulogne accompanied by 266 and 402 (Canadian) Squadrons. He shot down an Me109 at 14,000 feet in mid-Channel between Dover and Calais. That same day, he had received news of his promotion to flight lieutenant and that he was to command 'A' Flight of the newly formed No. 452 (Australian) Squadron at Kirton-in-Lindsey.

On 13th May, good news arrived that he was to be awarded the Distinguished Flying Cross. His citation read:

This officer has shown great keenness in his efforts to engage the enemy and he has destroyed at least five of their aircraft. His courage and enthusiasm have been a source of encouragement to other pilots of the squadron.

By 21st May, 452 had received their Spitfire Mk IIs and Finucane had the emblem of the Irish Shamrock painted in green on to the left hand front panel of his aircraft.

Leading the squadron in offensive sweeps over Northern France he accounted for another aircraft destroyed on 11th July, five miles west of Lille at 3.00 pm, shooting down a Me109, the pilot managed to bale-out. He was ordered to take the squadron to Kenley on 21st July and form the all-Spitfire Wing with 602 (City of Glasgow) and 485 (New Zealand) Squadrons.

Heavily involved over the next three months in action against the Luftwaffe, between August and October his score increased immensely that by 13th October 1941, Finucane had destroyed 16 Messerschmitt 109s, two probably destroyed, two shared and two damaged. In September, he was awarded a Bar to his DFC on 9th and received a second Bar on 26th. That October he was given the award of the Distinguished Service Order on 21st of that month. His citation for the award of the DSO stated the following:

Recently during two sorties on consecutive days, Flight Lieutenant Finucane destroyed five Messerschmitt 109s bringing his total victories to 20. He has flown with this squadron since June 1941, during which time the squadron has destroyed 42 enemy aircraft of which Flight Lieutenant Finucane has personally destroyed 15. The success achieved is undoubtedly due to this officer's brilliant leadership and example.

In November 1941, Brendan Finucane had become the top scoring pilot in RAF Fighter Command's No. 11 Groups list of aces.

During a night on the town to Croydon's Greyhound pub with other members of his squadron, and on heading home, Finucane eager to relieve himself from the evening's excess of beer, and jumped a wall at the Croydon Town Hall, only to find that the drop the other side was of eighteen feet. He landed on his right ankle and immediately felt an agonising pain. He was rushed to the Sutton Emergency Hospital where after having an x-ray; he had suffered a hairline fracture in his right heel bone. His foot was put into plaster and he was ordered to rest. It would not be until January 1942, that he was given the OK to return to flying. On return to Kenley on 19th January, he was promoted to squadron leader and given command of 602 Squadron based at the satellite airfield at Redhill.

It was on 20th February that Finucane almost came to grief whilst on a flight accompanied by another Spitfire over to Dunkirk at 10.55 am. Flying low over the Channel, they spotted and strafed a small enemy vessel, but as they flew along the French coast they encountered two German aircraft, the new Focke-Wulf 190s. The 190s had a more powerful engine than the Spitfire Mk Vs and before Finucane could get into a firing position his Spitfire was hit and bullets which caused a shard of metal to embed into his right thigh. He contacted his fellow pilot and told him he had been hit and was heading home. His colleague Dick Lewis kept a watchful eye on him as they made their way back.

At one stage Finucane seemed to lose control, when his Spitfires wing began to drop. He made his way back to Kenley and on taxing into the dispersal, came to a halt before losing consciousness. He was rushed to Horton Hospital, where he was operated on to remove the metal from his leg. He did not return to Kenley until 10th March. Between 13th March and 8th June 1942, he accounted for another 8 enemy aircraft destroyed, 3 probably destroyed and 4 damaged.

Finucane was again promoted on 21st June 1942 to Wing Commander Flying at the age of just 21 years old and given command of the Hornchurch Wing, this consisted of 64, 81 and 154 and 122 Squadron based at Fairlop. He led the Wing on a number of sweeps and provided fighter escort to a bomber raid on Hazelbrouck.

On 15th July 1942, the Wing was scheduled for a Ramrod mission (an attack by fighter aircraft only with machine guns and cannon) against the German Army camp at Etaples near Le Touquet. At 12.55 pm, as they made landfall over Le Touquet, flying low over the beach, Finucane's Spitfire was hit by a bullet from a German machine gun on the ground. His Spitfire immediately began to stream white glycol vapour from his holed radiator. His wingman, Alan Aikman called up to his leader saying 'I think you've had it Sir, in your radiator.'

Finucane had no choice but to turn his aircraft around and try and make for home. When only ten miles out from the French coast, he decided he would have to ditch his Spitfire into the Channel. He throttled back and prepared to land in the water. According to Aikman, he made the perfect landing, but almost immediately the Spitfire began to sink and within seconds Brendan Finucane disappeared. Aikman remained over where Finucane had ditched, but no sign of his commander could be seen; he sent out a mayday signal, and other aircraft from the Wing circled for ten minutes before shortage of fuel forced them to head for home. One theory is that Finucane had undone his cockpit seat Sutton harness and that on ditching, he had been thrown forward and knocked unconscious on the gun-sight. So ended the life of one of the RAF's most talented fighter pilots and leaders.

His death made headline news and his family were inundated with letters from the public expressing sympathy. Air Marshal Sholto-Douglas, Commander-in-Chief of Fighter Command sent a message to the Finucane family in which he wrote:

Your son's courage, skill and powers of leadership were a great inspiration to the Fighter Command, including myself. His influence among his fellow pilots was remarkable for one of his age. We will miss him greatly. He was the beau ideal of the 'fighter boy.'

He is remembered on the Runnymede Memorial, Panel 64. His score at the time of his death of enemy aircraft shot down stood at 26 and 6 shared destroyed, 8 and 1 shared probable, 8 damaged.

Franklin Road – Pilot Officer William Henry Franklin DFM*

Born in Poplar in the East End of London on 2nd October 1911, William Henry Franklin, the son of George and Harriet Franklin nee Parker, was delivered at the family home at No. 396 Commercial Road. His father was a general labourer who worked in the Mile End area. The family then moved to 65 Roswell Street in Bow.

It was a difficult childhood and needy time being brought up in the streets and roads around the East End. But there was some escape in being interested in various modes of transports of which the young boy was keen. He was educated at the Thomas Street Central School in Limehouse and was an enthusiastic pupil. He left school after four years with a glowing testimonial in the studies of mathematics, science, technical drawing and wood and metal workshop practice. On leaving school he worked for a short time for a chemist to be tutored in the practice, but he found it humdrum and did not excite his mind. Deciding this profession was not for him; Franklin's next decision was to join the Territorial Army with the Royal Artillery on a one years' service.

He enlisted as a gunner of 337th Battery (Territorial Army) Essex F. Battalion, Royal Artillery on 31st January 1928. By July, he had been appointed as a driver, but he had already other thoughts on his mind, when he was discharged on 14th January 1929.

He decided that after seeing an advertisement for recruitment into the Royal Air Force, that this might be the exciting and interesting career that he was seeking. Franklin enlisted as a boy aircraft apprentice on 15th January 1929 and was sent to the RAF School at RAF Halton in Buckinghamshire to learn his trade. He excelled in his new role and was part of No. 4 Wing. He was then offered by the RAF a twelve year regular service, which he accepted starting from 2nd October 1929. He was then placed under training to become a fitter on aero engines in January 1930 and after completing the course was reclassified as a Leading Aircraftsman on 15th January 1932 at the Fighter Establishment with No. 58 Squadron at Worthy Down.

The squadron was then posted overseas on 18th October 1933 to Iraq, where the squadron undertook operations against tribal unrest within the country.

'Bill' Franklin as he became known to his colleagues, re-mustered as a part-time gunner during this period and by March 1935 was posted to 84 Squadron at Shaibah.

By this time, he was determined that his future was that of a pilot. Four months later on 11th July, he was undergoing pilot training at No. 4 Flying Training School at Abu Sueir. Here he learnt to fly on Avro 504 and Avro Tutor biplanes. After going solo and gaining his wings, he was promoted to sergeant on 3rd April 1936 and posted to No. 64 Squadron at Ismailia, that same month. Five months later the squadron returned to Britain and was based at Martlesham Heath, Suffolk, where on 21st April 1937, Franklin was posted to 79 Squadron at Biggin Hill, Kent.

His stay was only brief and he received instructions to join No. 65 Squadron at Hornchurch on 1st June 1937. The squadron was commanded by Squadron Leader C.F.H. Grace and was in the process of exchanging their old Gloster Gauntlet aircraft for the new Gloster Gladiator. Franklin soon made friends at Hornchurch amongst his fellow sergeant pilots some of whom had also trained at RAF Halton as apprentices.

Before he had joined the RAF, he had struck up a relationship with a local young woman named Louise Kogel and eventually they had fallen in love. They now decided to marry and did so at the All Saint's Church, Poplar. They then moved into a brand new house at Elm Park, Hornchurch. It was quite an achievement in those days for a young man in his twenties to buy his own home. They now resided at No. 504 Orchard Avenue later renamed Calbourne Avenue.

Unfortunately the days of peace were numbered and the threat of war with Nazi Germany loomed on the horizon. In March 1939, 65 Squadron replaced their out of date biplanes for the new eight-gun

Supermarine Spitfires that had now become available. The pilots spent many hours honing their skills in the new aircraft that they would later need against the Germans.

Franklin's first action against the Germans, like so many who flew at that time from Hornchurch would be during the Dunkirk operation to rescue the retreating British troops over in France. His first patrol over Dunkirk was uneventful, but on the following day of 22nd May 1940, when during an early afternoon, he sighted a single Ju88 off Calais at 4,000 feet. His flight commander Gerald Saunders fired first at the enemy aircraft, but overshot. Franklin was able to manoeuvre his Spitfire on to the bombers tail and fired a two second burst, which seemed to have hit the pilot as the aircraft began to stagger badly. He fired another burst from his machine guns and this caused the enemy's starboard engine to stop. The Germans did not return fire and Franklin last saw the Junkers heading down into cloud, smoking badly. On returning to base, he claimed a half share on the Ju 88 as damaged.

As the operation continued, Franklin was in the thick of the action; from 24th to 28th May, he claimed another two enemy aircraft destroyed and four half shared destroyed.

There was a lull in air operations from early June as Britain waited for Hitler and his army's next move. The planned invasion of Britain code-named 'Operation Sealion' was being prepared.

Bill Franklin's next victory over the enemy came on 25th June, when the squadron engaged Messerschmitt 109s over northern France. Taking off at 4.25 pm on an offensive patrol, the nine Spitfires headed out across the Channel and just north of Abbeville they intercepted twelve 109s at 15,000 feet. Franklin's combat report gave details of his action:

We attacked per section. An enemy aircraft circled on to my sections tail and I immediately broke away to engage, but Blue 3 got there before me. I was attacked by two Me109s and so turned sharply to get on the tail of one. I manoeuvred into position behind his tail and fired a short burst of fire from my guns at 200 yards range. The aircraft burst into flames and dived vertically. I was then engaged by a second enemy aircraft. I latched on to his tail, as the other Germans attacked me from the rear. I broke away and after considerable manoeuvring, had lost height at 4,000 feet.

One Me109 attacked again from behind, but I was able to turn slightly and get on to his tail. I followed him down as he turned and seeing me closing on him, he half rolled. This brought the other two enemy aircraft out of position for an attack on me. I followed inside the first aircraft and fired short bursts at 250-yards and witnessed the Messerschmitt dive into the ground.

Franklin broke off his attack and headed swiftly for home. On return to Hornchurch, he claimed the two Messerschmitts as destroyed. He claimed two more 109s on 7th July and another on 8th July. The very next day, he learned that he had been awarded the Distinguished Flying Medal for his outstanding actions against the enemy. The squadron Operations Book reported:

We seem to be getting more action nowadays and Flight Sergeant Franklin is enjoying himself thoroughly, we hope he keeps up the good work. How about more decorations?

During August 1940, he increased his number of victories steadily; on 5th August he destroyed a Me109 and damaged two others and on 16th August destroyed an Me109, and damaged another and damaged a Dornier 17 bomber. He was also awarded a Bar to his DFM and promoted to the rank of pilot officer.

At the end of August, the squadron was posted to Turnhouse in Scotland for a rest period. They had lost seven pilots killed during the battle. They remained here for the next two months and spent time training up new replacements. During this period Bill Franklin was given leave and was able to visit his family down south. During the end of November 1940, 65 Squadron was sent south again with orders to operate from RAF Tangmere near Chichester in Sussex.

During a winter's afternoon on 12th December, 'B' Flight led by Squadron Leader Saunders took off from Tangmere and proceeded in the direction of Selsey Bill and sighted a lone Junkers Ju88. Blue Section manoeuvred into a line astern formation to attack. The German bomber replied firing its twin cannon and then dived steeply towards the French coast and into cloud. Sergeant Lawson managed to get close enough to fire off a two second burst, but in spite of this the Junkers escaped.

It then was noticed that both Bill Franklin and Sergeant Merrick Hine were nowhere to be seen. It was reported that a Spitfire had been seen to break up and dive into the sea. Although the area was searched by the rest of the squadron and search and rescue was notified, no trace of either pilot or his aircraft was found. They were both presumed killed and listed as missing in action. It was presumed that both pilots had followed the German into cloud and had been shot down.

His wife Louise was devastated by his loss, but remained loyal to his memory until her own death in 1975. She was invited to attend Buckingham Palace in 1941 to receive from King George VI the Distinguished Flying Medal and Bar. It was a proud, but sad moment for her to be given her late husband's award. Bill Franklin was aged 29 years when he was lost in action. Today, he is remembered at the Runnymede Memorial on Panel 8 as well as the road in Hornchurch. He was one of the ace pilots of 1940.

Freeborne Gardens – Wing Commander John Freeborn DFC*

(Please note the street sign misspelt with extra e added)

Born in Middleton, Yorkshire on 1st December 1919, John Connell Freeborn was one of three brothers and two sisters of Harold and Jean Freeborn. His father was a bank manager for the Yorkshire Penny Bank and strict disciplinarian as to bringing up his family; and they attended church every Sunday.

The family moved from Middleton to Headingly in the 1920s and John was educated at the Leeds Grammar School until the age of sixteen and on leaving was still undecided to what profession he would go into. His choice was either to join the armed services or work in the local industries of coal or the railways. At the age of seventeen he joined the Reserve of Air Force Officers after reading of the events that had taken place in Abyssinia, when the dictator Benito Mussolini had his troops invade the country. Freeborn felt that something should be done to halt the killing and misery being inflicted on the African people. John was a typical Yorkshire man, who was straight talking and expressed his views forthright, he maintained this ideal right through his life and could not stand 'bullshit.'

Having been accepted into the RAFO, he was sent to the Elementary Flying Training School at Sywell on 17th January 1938, where he learnt on Tiger Moth biplanes. The course lasted three months and Freeborn was rated as above average having gone solo with just 4-hours and 20-minutes flying training. He was then sent up to Montrose to No. 8 FTS for more flying experience on 9th April, this time on Hawker Hart aircraft.

On completion of this course, he was an acting pilot officer and posted to join No. 74 Squadron at Hornchurch on 29th October 1938. Arriving at Hornchurch, he was introduced to the squadron commander Squadron Leader George Sampson and then taken to 'B' Flight, where he met its flight commander Paddy Treacy. He settled in

79

to his new life at the aerodrome which had all the luxuries of a peacetime station, guest evenings in the officers' mess, flying the squadron's Gloster Gauntlet aircraft on Empire Air Days and undertaking air exercises. In January 1939, he was made pilot officer and one month later the squadron became the second unit in the RAF to be re-equipped with the new Spitfire aeroplane.

With the threat of war now imminent in the autumn of 1939, the squadron was put on a war footing and when war was declared on 3rd September, the pilots were 'at readiness.' Three days into the war on 6th September, Freeborn became involved in an incident that would haunt him for the rest of his life.

Radar had picked up an unidentified aircraft coming in across the North Sea and 74 Squadron was scrambled to locate and intercept. Freeborn and others led by Flight Commander 'Sailor' Malan sighted some aircraft over the West Mersea Estuary and were ordered to attack. Freeborn and his colleague Paddy Byrne dived down to attack. Unfortunately, the two aircraft were Hawker Hurricanes on patrol from North Weald, but within a few seconds both Hurricanes had been shot down, with one of the pilots being killed. On landing back at Hornchurch both Freeborn and Byrne were placed under open arrest. An inquiry was launched and both pilots were sent to stand before a General Court Marshall on 29th October 1939.

Fortunately they were both acquitted after the circumstances of the tragic incident were told. This was to become known in RAF circles as the 'Battle of Barking Creek.'

Freeborn returned to the squadron and in May 1940 was heavily involved in action during Dunkirk. His first German aircraft claimed on 21st May, when he probably destroyed a Junkers Ju88 bomber and another the following day, ten miles north of Calais. On 27th, he claimed one Messerschmitt 109 destroyed and another unconfirmed.

The squadron was sent to Leaconfield following Dunkirk for a rest period, but they returned to Hornchurch on 6th June 1940.

In July, during the Battle of Britain, 74 Squadron was sent down every morning to RAF Manston in Kent, to operate from. During the intense fighting against the hordes of Luftwaffe bombers and fighters, Freeborn steadily notched up an impressive score against the enemy, destroying seven German aircraft and damaging another. He was delighted to learn of his winning the Distinguished Flying Cross on 31st August 1940. His DFC Citation said:

This officer has taken part in nearly all offensive patrols carried out by his squadron since the commencement of the war, including operations over the Low Countries and Dunkirk, and more recently, engagements over the Channel and south-eastern England. During this period of intensive air warfare, he has destroyed four enemy aircraft. His high courage and exceptional abilities as a leader have materially contributed to the notable success and high standard of efficiency maintained by the squadron.

On 3rd September 1940, while based at Coltishall, Freeborn was raised in rank to that of flying officer and made a flight commander. That day, accompanied by his mother, he went to Buckingham Palace to receive his DFC from His Majesty the King. During November he claimed another 109 destroyed and on 5th December shot down two 109s shared in the destruction of another and damaged a fourth.

He was now the longest serving operational pilot on the squadron and flown the largest amount of hours. Freeborn received the award of a Bar to his DFC on 25th February. He remained with 74 Squadron into 1941 until he was posted away as an instructor to No. 57 Operational Flying Unit at RAF Hawarden to train pilots on Spitfires on 6th June. He was promoted in rank to flight lieutenant on 3rd September 1941.

He remained at Hawarden until December 1941 before was posted to 145 Squadron at Catterick, but this was short lived and within a week of joining this unit, he found his next appointment was to visit the United States as a liaison officer following America's entry into the war after the attack at Pearl Harbor.

While there, he was able to pass on valuable information to new pilots regarding combat at the air bases in Alabama, he also got the chance to fly some of the American aircraft. He remained in the USA until December 1942 and on return to Britain returned to fly operations again as a flight commander with No. 602 'City of Glasgow' Squadron based at Skeabra.

During his time with this squadron he undertook many escort operations on bomber raids against German installations and shipping on the Dutch and French coasts; the squadron moved to operate from Perranporth in Cornwall and then to Lasham, near Andover in Hampshire.

He stayed with 602 until he was posted to command 118 Squadron at Coltishall in Norfolk on 17th June 1943. Again operations consisted of escorting British or American bombers on raids over Europe. By August the squadron was sent north, firstly to Peterhead then to Castletown in Scotland. Freeborn was promoted to the rank of temporary squadron leader on 1st January 1944, and full rank on 30th April. He was to become the RAFs youngest Wing Commander Flying when he was given command of 286 Wing in June 1944, based at Grottaglie in southern Italy.

The Wing was heavily involved not only in offensive operations in that area of campaign, but in also protection against the Allied shipping and re-enforcements being pushed to the front as the Allies advanced further into Italy and the Balkans.

Without a break in operations for eighteen months, Freeborn was feeling fatigued and he was prompted to return to Britain for a well-earned rest. Following his rest period, he was sent to the OTU at Tern Hill as the chief flying instructor, then to Hawarden before his final posting to RAF Netheravon on 8th December 1944. He remained with this unit until the end of the war.

Freeborn resigned from the Royal Air Force in 1946; during his service he had flown 42-different types of aircraft, become an ace with a final score of 11 and 2 shared destroyed, 3 and 1 shared unconfirmed destroyed, 1 probable and 1 and 3 shared damaged.

After the war, he trained and became a qualified driving instructor, but soon after joined the Tetley Walker Company as Regional Director for their Minister Minerals soft drinks brand. In his own personal life, he had married Rita Fielder in 1944 and they had one daughter, Julia. His wife died in 1979, and he took early retirement and moved to Spain. It was in Spain that he met Margaret Ena (known as Peta) and they fell in love and married in 1983. They returned to Britain to live, Peta sadly passed away in 2001. John Freeborn died at the Formby Hospital on 28th August 2010 aged 90 years.

Gillam Way – Group Captain Denys Gillam DSO** DFC*

Denys Edgar Gillam was born at Tynemouth, Tyne and Wear on 18th November 1915. He was educated at Bramcote Boarding School in Scarborough and then at Wrekin College in Shropshire. There is little information regarding Gillam's life after leaving college, but at some point he learnt to fly and obtained his pilots' licence at the Public School Aviation Camp, Norfolk in September 1934; joining the RAF on a short service commission as an acting pilot officer on April 16th 1935 and being sent to No. 6 FTS at Netheravon for training on May 7th. On completion of this course he was posted to his first squadron, No.29 stationed at North Weald, Essex on 6th March 1936. After serving for nine months with this squadron he was transferred to the Meteorological Flight at Aldergrove in Northern Ireland in January 1937.

It was while serving here that he undertook two perilous flights to drop food supplies to the islanders of Rathlin Island situated just off County Antrim, which had been cut-off from the mainland that June due to heavy gales. He had flown the much needed food in a Westland Wapiti biplane which was quite outdated at that time. For this, he was awarded the Air Force Cross on 9th June 1938.

He received news that he was to be posted to a fighter squadron in September 1939 and joined No. 616 'South Yorkshire' Auxiliary

Squadron based at Finningley, near Doncaster on 18th September. They were equipped with Spitfires in October after moving to Leconfield.

The squadron was declared operational by early 1940 and were moved south to the Hornchurch Sector to operate during the Dunkirk Evacuation in mid-May 1940. They were sent to Rochford airfield, near Southend on 27th and from here, on 1st June he claimed his first success of the war, when he damaged a Junkers Ju88 bomber over Dunkirk. The Squadron moved back to Leconfield and from here they flew during July until mid-August.

On 15th August, Gillam added another Ju88 to his score, before moving to RAF Kenley, where on 26th August he shot down a Messerschmitt 109 and a day later a Messerschmitt 110. His shooting skills were excellent on the 30thAugust, destroying an Me109, one probably destroyed and two others damaged. On 1st September, he shot down one Dornier 17 bomber with another probably destroyed and third damaged and a Messerschmitt 109. The next day, he was in action once again and destroyed a Messerschmitt 110, but his luck ran out, when his Spitfires engine was set alight by return enemy fire and he was obliged to bale-out over Maidstone. He floated down and landed without injury into the sea and was picked up by an air sea rescue launch. This was his last action with 616 Squadron, as on 6th September he received notification of promotion as a flight commander and posting to the Czech Squadron, No.312 based at Speke.

On October 8th 1940, Gillam was to enter the record books, when accompanied by two Czech pilots; they were hurriedly scrambled at 4.10 pm, as German bombers arrived near to the airfield. No sooner had the three Hurricanes become airborne, than they sighted a Junkers Ju88 bomber directly ahead and climbing; both Czech pilots attacked in turn and Gillam was able to attack it from the stern. All three Hurricanes were hit by return fire from the German aircraft. The Junkers was badly damaged and was forced to land in a field. Gillam landed back at Speke airfield with his two comrades, the sortie from start to finish only taking eleven minutes in total. The quickest combat victory recorded of the war. He then drove his car to the scene of the enemy aircraft's crash and found that three of the Germans had been captured, some with injuries, but the observer had been killed.

On 12th November, Gillam was awarded the Distinguished Flying Cross, the citation stated:

This officer has been responsible for the destruction of seven enemy aircraft and probably of four more, and has damaged six. On one occasion during a combat with a large force of Messerschmitt 110s, he shot one down and his own aircraft caught fire. He descended by parachute and returned to his station in time to lead the next patrol. On another occasion Flight Lieutenant Gillam shot down a Junkers 88 and landed within eleven minutes from the time he took off.

Following his award of the DFC in November, on 1st December 1940, Gillam was promoted to temporary squadron leader and was posted to command No. 306 (Polish) Squadron at Tern Hill. His stay with this unit was only short for on 2nd March 1941; he was posted to Headquarters 9 Group and remained there until July 9th, when he returned to operations as commanding officer with 615 Squadron then based at Anglesey, they then moved to Manston that September to undertake anti-shipping sorties. During one operation on 9th October, Gillam claimed the destruction of two Heinkel 59 floatplanes caught on the water. The award of a Bar to his DFC was given on 21st October.

In another operation on 23rd November, his aircraft was hit by German ground fire over Dunkirk and he was wounded in both legs and arms; although hurt he managed to bale-out and upon landing in the sea, inflated his survival dinghy. His colleagues circled him until an air sea rescue launch arrived and picked him up. The award of the Distinguished Service Order was gazetted on 12th December 1941. Following recovery from his wounds, Gillam was sent to America in January 1942 to give a series of lectures to American aircrews, this lasted until March and on his return, he was posted to RAF Duxford to form the first Hawker Typhoon Wing. The wing flew its first operational mission over Dieppe on 19th August, during the combined services raid on the coastal port.

In October, he was posted to attend the RAF Staff College and following this course, he was sent to work at Headquarters No. 12 Group in February 1943. In August that year, he returned to the United States and was sent to the Command and General Staff School at Fort Leavenworth, Kansas. He remained there for three months and on return to Britain was made Wing Leader of 146 Wing in December 1943. In April 1944, Gillam took over command of 20 Sector 2nd Tactical Air Force, and in July was given command of 146 Wing. The award of a Bar to his DSO came on 11th August 1944.

During a raid against high-ranking German officers on 24th October, Gillam led his Wing against a fortified building at Dordrecht in southern Holland. Diving down from an altitude of 6,000 feet, he placed marker bombs, followed by two 500-pound bombs. Five other Typhoons also came in low and dropped their bombs. The result of the attack was the death of two generals, 17-senior officers and 55-officers of the German Fifteenth Army. The award of a second Bar to his DSO was given on 23rd January 1945. This citation read:

Since being awarded a bar to the DSO, Group Captain Gillam has completed more than 80 sorties, involving attacks on the enemy troop and tank concentrations, ammunition stores, locomotives and other targets on the ground. Within recent weeks, he has led formations of aircraft against several important and heavily defended targets. These missions called for a degree of skill and resolution and the success achieved is a splendid tribute to this officer's outstanding leadership and ability. He has set an example of the very high order.

Gillam was posted to Headquarters 84 Group as Group Captain Ops in February 1945 and following the end of the war in Europe in May and the Far East in August, was sent to 84 Group Disbandment

Centre. He was released from the Royal Air Force that October. Denys Gillam re-joined his first squadron No. 616 Auxiliary Air Force as a flight lieutenant in 1946. During peacetime, he became a successful businessman with his own carpet firm and also owned a farm in North Yorkshire. He became the Deputy Lieutenant of West Riding of Yorkshire and the City and County of York in 1959. He was also a director of the Hanfrey & Company Limited between 1950 till 1981 and was their chairman between 1971 and 1981, after which he retired. He died in September 1991

Gilroy Close – Group Captain George Gilroy DSO, DFC,* DFC (US)

Born on 1st June 1914 at the family home of 'Kingledores' near Edinburgh, George Kemp Gilroy was an only son. He became a sheep farmer and breeder and involved in the country pastimes of shooting and became an exceptional marksman. His friends nicknamed him 'Sheep' which would remain into his RAF career. At some stage an interest in flying came to the fore and he learnt to fly at the Edinburgh Flying Club at Macmerry in East Lothian and then joined No. 603 Auxiliary Squadron as an acting pilot officer on 10th November 1938. He was called up to full-time service on 23rd August 1939, just a few weeks before the outbreak of war.

Gilroy was to become one of the first RAF pilots of the war to engage the enemy, when on 16th October 1939, German bombers made an attack against British warships anchored in the Forth Estuary. Attacking a Junkers Ju88 bomber with two other Spitfires in attendance, his aircraft was hit by return fire from the German gunner and on landing he found one bullet hole in the engine cowling. Two of the German aircraft were shot down, 603 Squadron claiming the first German aircraft of the war. Twelve days later on 28th October, he was able to share in the destruction of a Heinkel 111 which was carrying out a long-range reconnaissance mission over the Forth. The Heinkel was attacked and brought down by Spitfires of both No.602 and 603 Squadrons, finally crash-landing onto the hillside just east of the village of Humbie.

During the early part of 1940, the squadron was involved with numerous encounters with the enemy and Gilroy was steadily making his mark. From 19th January until 24th July, he shared in the destruction of three Heinkel 111s and two Dornier 17 aircraft.

The squadron was sent south to Hornchurch during the Battle of Britain in late August and immediately, Gilroy was in the thick of the action, shooting down a Messerschmitt 109 on 28th August and another two days later on 31st. On that day unfortunately, he was shot down in combat over London and was forced to take to his parachute. Floating down and landing in Hereford Road in Wanstead, he was immediately attacked by a crowd of people, thinking he was a German pilot. He was surrounded and began to take blows from the incensed crowd. He was saved by a bus conductress who had recognised his RAF blue shirt, as Gilroy had not been wearing his RAF tunic that day. Battered and bruised, he was taken to the King George Hospital in Ilford and treated for his injuries. So outraged was the Mayor of Dagenham, when he heard of Gilroy's incident, that he arranged for a cheque of £10.00 to be presented to him for the squadron to buy a round of drinks.

On 13th September, he received the award of the Distinguished Flying Cross. Throughout October and November he continued to add to his score with a Messerschmitt 109 destroyed on 28th October and a share in the destruction of a Heinkel on 21st November. However, on 17th December 1940, following the squadrons returned to RAF Drem in Scotland, 'Sheep' Gilroy was involved in a landing accident, when his Spitfires tail was hit by Sergeant Price's aircraft, which bounced into the air and crashed on top of his cockpit. A fellow pilot, David Scott-Malden in another aircraft that had just landed, ran over to Gilroy's aircraft and dragged him clear as the Spitfire's cockpit began to catch fire. He was taken to hospital with severe, but not life threatening injuries. Gilroy remained in hospital for

Alfred Adnams, pictured centre, was Station Commander at RAF Hornchurch 1943-44.

Douglas Bader flew briefly from Hornchurch in May 1940 with 222 Squadron.

Pilot Officer, the Right Honourable Walter Beaumont DFC.

George Bennions DFC, flew with No. 41 Squadron throughout the Battle of Britain.

Ronald 'Ras' Berry DSO, DFC, was a stalwart member of 603 Squadron.

Cecil 'Boy' Bouchier (centre), who was Station Commander throughout the Battle of Britain at Hornchurch.

Flight Lieutenant John Boulter of 603 Squadron.   Copyright David Ross.

Group Captain Harry Broadhurst was Commander at Hornchurch from 1941-42.

Ace pilot Brian Carbury from New Zealand.

Wing Commander William Crawford –
Compton 1943.

Al Deere of 54 Squadron became a legend
for surviving against the odds.

'Uncle' George Denholm, he led 603 Squadron
during 1940.

Robert Dewey paid the ultimate sacrifice in 1940, keeping Britain free from Nazi invasion.

Derek Dowding of 74 Squadron, his father ACM Hugh Dowding was Commander in Chief of Fighter Command during 1940.

Flying Officer Hilary Edridge of 222 Squadron.   Copyright Andy Saunders

Lieutenant Commander Eugene Esmonde VC, led the attack against the German battle cruiser Scharnhorst in 1942.

'Paddy' Finucane from Ireland, one of the most famous fighter pilots of WW2 flew from Hornchurch in 1940 and again in 1942.

'Bill' Franklin, pre-war pilot at Hornchurch, he became an ace during 1940, but was killed in action that year.

John Freeborn of 74 Squadron, he became an ace and flew more operational hours than any other pilot in the squadron.

Group Captain Denys Gillam DSO, DFC.

George Gilroy of 603 Squadron, known as 'Sheep' by his colleagues because of his early farming days.   Copyright David Ross

Colin Gray who served with 54 Squadron, went on to become the top-scoring New Zealand fighter ace of the war.

Sergeant Patrick Hayes of 65 Squadron was also a keen photographer. Sadly, he was killed just at the start of the Battle of Britain.
                    Copyright P.S. Hayes

Flight Lieutenant Ray Hesselyn, became an ace pilot not only in England, but also Malta.

Flying Officer Richard Hillary of 603 Squadron, whose wartime book of his time at Hornchurch in 1940, 'The Last Enemy' has become a classic. Copyright David Ross

Petrus 'Dutch' Hugo from South Africa became Wing Leader at Hornchurch in July 1942.

Wing Commander John 'Killy' Kilmartin fought during the battles of France and Britain before becoming Wing Leader at Hornchurch in 1943.

Wing Commander Don Kingaby, the only wartime pilot to be awarded three DFM medals.

Sergeant David Kirton was one of Hornchurch's early casualties during the Battle of Britain aged 21 years.

James Leathart of No.54 Squadron, known as 'Prof' because of his academic background.

Flight Lieutenant Eric Lock, top-scoring ace of the Battle of Britain with No. 41 Squadron.

Squadron Leader Tony Lovell of 41 Squadron flew more operations throughout the war than most pilots.

The legendary 'Sailor' Malan who started his flying career at RAF Hornchurch and went on to become perhaps the finest fighter pilot and leader of WW2.

'Tubby' Mermagen was the first commander of the newly re-formed 222 'Natal' Squadron.

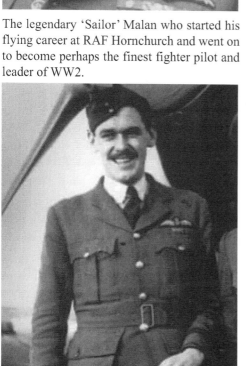

Flight Lieutenant John Mungo-Park of 74 Squadron, he teamed up with H.M. Stephen and became a formidable fighting team during 1940-41.

New Zealander Keith Park, first commander at RAF Hornchurch following its re-opening in 1928.

Flying Officer Peter Pease of 603 Squadron, his bravery and death in action was even commended by the Germans he had attacked in his Spitfire.   Copyright David Ross

William Leefe Robinson VC, the first pilot to shoot down a German airship over British soil in 1916.

Group Captain Norman Ryder DFC, flew with No. 41 Squadron throughout the Battle of Britain. He was later shot down to become a prisoner of war.

Sergeant Alfred Sarre of 603 Squadron, was shot down a number of times, but continued his fight against the enemy and mental stress.
Copyright David Ross

Wing Commander Peter Simpson DFC, was a Wing Leader at Hornchurch during 1943.

Frederick Sowrey DSO, MC was the second pilot from Hornchurch to shoot down a Zeppelin Airship in September 1916.

Frederick Stapleton became Wing Comander Flying at Hornchurch in 1941, and led the squadrons on many missions over the Channel.

Squadron Leader H.M. Stephen flew with 74 'Tiger' Squadron and achieved ace status. During one day in August 1940, he claimed 8 enemy aircraft.

Wulstan Tempest, of 39 Squadron was the third pilot from Hornchurch to bring down a Zeppelin in October 1916.

Robert Stanford Tuck joined Hornchurch pre-war and later was one of the top aces.

Edward 'Hawkeye' Wells, a New Zealander with exceptional eyesight and marksmanship in aerial combat, was to become a top ace.

The RAF Hornchurch Officers Mess pictured in 1937.

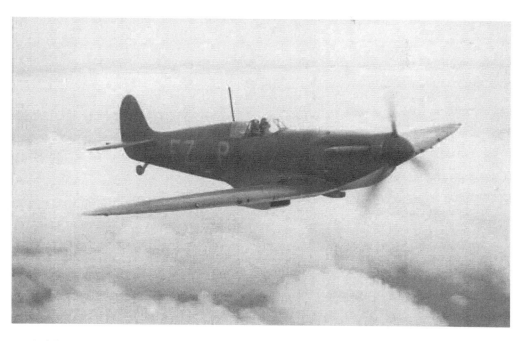

Spitfire of No. 65 Squadron in flight, photographed in early 1939 by pilot Patrick Hayes.

Three cheers for the King! Medal award presentation, Hornchurch, June 1940. L/R P/O J. Allen DFC, F/O Tuck DFC, P/O A. Deere DFC, F/Lt A. Malan DFC and F/Lt J. Leathart DSO.

Cut the cake Norman! F/Lt Norman Ryder of 41 Squadron cuts his birthday cake on 28th November 1940.

A Spitfire of No. 122 Squadron being checked over by maintenance crew, May 1942.

A Hornchurch Spitfire is refuelled ready for its next sortie.

An excellent photograph showing some of the flying kit worn by Fighter Command pilots during 1942.

Pilots of 122 Squadron at readiness 1942.

Return to Hornchurch 1960
L/R Ronald Adam, Colin Gray, 'Ras' Berry, Bob Tuck, film producer and Norman Ryder.

several weeks, he did not return to operations until the spring of 1941, when the squadron was operating Channel sweeps from Hornchurch. During this period, he claimed three more Me109s damaged.

On 29th July, Gilroy was given command of No. 609 'West Riding' Auxiliary Squadron based at Gravesend, Kent. With this unit, he claimed another three Me109s destroyed, one Focke-Wulf 190 and another damaged; the award of the Belgium Croix de Guerre was presented to him on 3rd March 1942. He was posted from 609 Squadron on 31st May. He was then rested from operations and did not return until he was posted to his next appointment in 325 Wing based in East Africa, but this was short lived as on 29th November 1942, he was sent to North Africa to command No. 324 Wing, which was pushing the German Afrika Corps back in retreat following the success at El Alamein the previous month.

Now flying Spitfire Mk Vbs, Gilroy damaged a Junkers Ju88 bomber on 30th November and a 109 on 6th December, on 16th December, he managed to destroy three Messerschmitts parked on the ground; two Heinkel He129s were also destroyed by him on 28th of that month.

At the start of January 1943 Gilroy added to his score with one enemy aircraft destroyed and two more shared. But tragedy struck on 28th January, when flying over Souk-el-Khemis, he collided with Flight Lieutenant Mortimer-Rose. Gilroy baled-out with slight injuries, but Mortimer-Rose was killed , when his aircraft spun in. On 2nd March 1943, he was awarded the Distinguished Service Order.

He carried on leading the Wing, including the invasion of Sicily (Operation 'Husky') in July 1943 and Italy on 3rd September. He was taken off operations in November and sent back to the United Kingdom and promoted to the rank of group captain; where he was then given command of the RAF Station at Wittering in No.12 Group. Later, he also commanded RAF Blakelaw in 13 Group. Gilroy was awarded the American DFC on 14th November 1944.

He was released from the Royal Air Force following the end of the war, but he re-joined the Auxiliary Squadron No. 603, becoming it's commanding officer from June 1946 until September 1949. He retired and took up sheep farming again in Scotland. He passed away in 1995.

Gray Gardens – Group Captain Colin Gray DSO, DFC**

Colin Falkland Gray was a New Zealander born with his twin brother Kenneth on 9th November 1914, at the family home in Christchurch. He was educated at Christ's College and became fascinated with aircraft and flying, whilst watching aeroplanes from the local airfield at Wigram. By the time he was about to leave full-time education, his wish was to join the Royal Air Force.

Managing to get an interview before a selection committee that was looking for Commonwealth recruits into the RAF; both Colin and Ken Gray were successful in applying and packed their belongings to sail for Britain. Ken sailing on 14th August 1937, but Colin because he had failed one of the medical tests, but succeeded in a re-test, he did not leave New Zealand until December 1938.

On arrival in Britain in January 1939, Gray was sent to No. 1 Elementary and Reserve Flying Training School at Hatfield in Hertfordshire. Here he learnt to fly on Tiger Moth biplanes and the course lasted until the end of March, when he received his civilian pilots 'A' Licence. He was then sent to the RAF Central Depot at Uxbridge for a two-week commissioning course, which on completion, he was made an 'acting pilot officer on probation.' Gray was then sent on a six-week service flying training course at RAF Shrewsbury, where he learnt to fly on single-engine Hawker Harts. Following successful completion of the course, he was delighted to find he had been selected to fly fighter aircraft and was sent to No. 11 Fighter Group Pool at St Athan in Glamorganshire.

Here he was trained on North American Harvard and Hawker Hurricane aeroplanes. At the end of November 1939, he received his first posting to a fighter squadron; No. 54 Squadron at Hornchurch.

No. 54 Squadron was equipped with Spitfire Mk1s; Gray flew his first operational sortie from Hornchurch on 17th December 1939, when he accompanied two other pilots to investigate an unidentified radar plot over the Channel, but nothing was seen. It was to be another six months before he would see action and fire his guns. Tragically, he received sad news on 1st May 1940, that his brother Ken had been killed, when his Whitely bomber had crashed into a hillside at Bains Hole, north-west of Dyce, near Aberdeen.

His first combat, took place during the evacuation of the Allied forces at Dunkirk in May 1940. On 24th May, he shot down his first enemy aircraft, two Messerschmitt 109s were claimed as probable destroyed; but he was himself on the receiving end that day, during the course of another combat, his Spitfire was badly damaged and his air speed indicator, flaps, guns and brakes all became inoperative. He managed to land his Spitfire back at Hornchurch aerodrome and on inspection found that the main elevator cables were hanging by threads; he was lucky that the whole tail-section had not blown off.

A report of the damage was sent to Vickers Supermarine, who were surprised and impressed with the amount of damage sustained to their aircraft, and that it kept flying, that they sent a local photographer to take photographs of the Spitfire.

With a brief respite in June, the Battle of Britain started in earnest in July and Gray with his keen eye and excellent marksmanship was soon increasing his tally of enemy aircraft. Between July 13th and 3rd September 1940, he claimed 15 aircraft destroyed, 4 probably destroyed and 8 damaged. He was now one of the top scoring aces and was awarded the DFC on 15th August 1940. Strangely, Colin Gray was not to see the citation for his award until nearly forty years later, when documents at the Public Records Office at Kew became available. The citation read:

Since 21st May 1940, Pilot Officer Gray has flown continuously with his squadron on offensive patrols. He took part in numerous engagements against the enemy throughout the Dunkirk operations, and subsequently throughout intensive air operations over the Kentish coast and in protection of shipping in the Channel. He has shot down four Messerschmitt 109s and it is believed, destroyed a further four. He also assisted in destroying one Messerschmitt 109 and one Dornier 215. This young and gallant officer is one of the few members of this hard pressed squadron who has survived the Dunkirk operations, and the subsequent intensive air operations. His example, courage and determination in action have contributed materially in maintaining the high morale of his squadron.

Although 54 Squadron had claimed many German aircraft, they had also suffered many casualties and by the end of August they were relieved and sent north to Catterick in Yorkshire for a period of rest. Gray was posted from 54 Squadron with promotion to flight lieutenant on 15th December 1940, and sent to 43 Squadron based at Drem in Scotland.

His stay with this squadron was only brief and he returned to 54 Squadron as a flight commander on 22nd January 1941. No. 54 returned to their old base at Hornchurch in February and carried out offensive sweeps across the Channel. Gray remained here until 12th June, when he was sent to No.1 Squadron based at Redhill, Surrey as 'B' Flight commander flying Hurricane Mk IIs. During his time at Redhill, he shared in the shooting down of a Heinkel 59 ten miles off Folkestone on 16th June and later flying a Spitfire coded EB-F with 41 Squadron on 22nd August, he shot down a Me109 which crashed at the airfield of Le Havre. On 20th September, he was awarded a Bar to his DFC.

Gray was posted to Debden on 28th September to take over command of 403 (Canadian) Squadron, but he was recalled to Tangmere three days later and given command of No. 616 Squadron at Westhampnett near Chichester. He remained with 616 until February 25th 1942, when he was posted to Headquarters 9 Group at Preston in Lancashire as Squadron Leader Tactics. 9 Group was a fighter group responsible for the air defence of the area west of the

Pennines, including Shropshire, Lancashire, North Wales and the Isle of Man.

In June, Gray was informed that American pilots would be arriving to convert on to Spitfires and that his job was to teach them battle tactics. He remained at 9 Group until he was posted to 485 (New Zealand) Squadron, he arrived at their base at Kings Cliffe on 15th September 1942 and remained with them until he was sent to 64 Squadron at Fairlop in Essex on 28th September as a supernumerary, where he flew several combat missions escorting American B17 Flying Fortresses and Liberators on raids in Northern France. Gray took over command of the squadron on 31st October from Squadron Leader Tony Gaze, an Australian.

On 26th December 1942, He was posted once more as a Tactics Officer to No.333 Group at Algiers in Tunisia, arriving there on 19th January, but then received news that he had been given command of the Spitfire Squadron No.81 which was re-equipping with Mk IX aircraft at Gibraltar and then flew to their operational base at Tingley airfield at Bone Algeria. In action over Tunisia with the squadron, Gray increased his score of enemy aircraft, destroying five including an Italian Macchi C.202.

He was awarded the Distinguished Service Order on 15th May 1943 and on June 1st was posted as Wing Commander Flying of No. 322 Wing at Ta Kali in Malta. Here the Allies were preparing for the invasion of Sicily, Gray's Wing consisting of five squadrons, 81, 152, 154, 232 and 242. The Allied landings against Sicily took place on 9th July and eight beaches were designated as landing points, Gray's Wing was to protect the landings at two of them code-named 'Cent' and 'Acid.' During the afternoon following the landings, Gray took off with 154 Squadron to patrol over the beaches and they were bounced by German fighter aircraft, Gray attacked one of the Messerschmitt 109s and recalled later:

I fired at the first one from 400-yards closing to 300, hitting him in the starboard wing and fuselage. There was a large explosion and many pieces fell off, and the plane burst into flames.

Between June and the end of July, he added another five aircraft to his score and was then posted back to Britain on 2nd October after completing two tours of duty, where he returned briefly to HQ 9 Group before being made Officer Commanding No. 2 Central Training Wing at Balado, in Scotland on 30th October 1943. He was awarded a second Bar to his DFC on 15th November and then posted to the Training Wing No.61 Operational Conversion Unit at Rednal, Shropshire on 4th December. Here he was in charge of flying and ground programmes for pilots converting to Spitfires for the operational squadrons.

He remained there until he was posted to the Fighter Leader's School at Milfield on June 8th 1944 as Officer Commanding the Spitfire Wing and from there was promoted to wing commander at Detling before going on to lead the Lympne Wing on 11th August 1944. Here he had four squadrons, No.41, 130, 350 and 610. The operations during this time consisted of sweeps, anti-buzz bomb defence, and they also provided escort during Operation 'Market Garden' in September, when the Allies launched the largest aerial parachute drop against the bridges at Arnhem and Nijmegen in Holland.

His final wartime posting was to RAF Skeabrae in the Orkney Islands on 2nd February 1945. As officer commanding the aerodrome provided defence for the Royal Navy at Scapa Flow and the Shetlands.

Post war, Colin Gray returned to New Zealand briefly and married Betty Cook on 20th October 1945 at Waerenga-a-hika, Gisborne. He remained in the RAF and served in various positions including British Joint Services Mission, Washington as Air 1- Liaison Officer with Headquarters United States Air Force in January 1950. In March 1954, he was posted to command RAF Church Fenton in Yorkshire as Acting Group Captain, in charge of three Meteor jet squadrons. His final post was at the Air Ministry in London in February 1959, in the Department of Assistant Chief of Air Staff, Air Defence, and later ACAS Operations who were responsible for operational aspects of all manned fighter aircraft and the control and reporting systems.

Gray finally decided to resign from the Royal Air Force in 1961 and that April, he and his family returned to New Zealand. Here, he joined the firm of Unilever and retired as a deputy director at the age of sixty-five. He lived the remainder of his life in Waikanae.

Colin Gray's final score of enemy aircraft destroyed made him the top-scoring New Zealand pilot of the Second World War with 27 and 2 shared destroyed, 6 and 4 shared probably destroyed and 12 damaged. He died on 1st August 1995 aged 80 years.

Hayes Drive – Sergeant Patrick Hayes

Patrick Sherlock Hayes was born on 17th March 1916 and was educated at King's College, Taunton, Devon in September 1930 until 1932, whereupon he entered into special training in London for banking. He joined the Midland Bank and became a member of the Midland Bank Flying Club. Having achieved his civilian pilot's license, he underwent training with the Royal Air Force Volunteer Reserve in May 1939. On finishing his course, he was then posted to No. 65 Squadron at Hornchurch. He was also a keen photographer and was able to take many photographs during his time at the aerodrome. Some of these appeared in the book 'Second to None' published by this author in 2004.

As a sergeant pilot, he took part in many patrols during the early part of the war, especially, during the evacuation at Dunkirk. Here he claimed one destroyed and one Dornier as a probable.

During the evening of Sunday 7th July 1940, Hayes accompanied by two other Spitfire pilots, Flying Officer George Proudman and Flying Officer Brisbane took off from Hornchurch to carry out a convoy patrol at 8.15 pm. Flying Spitfire N3129, Hayes and his fellow pilots

95

were attacked by Messerschmitt 109s of 6/JG51 over Folkestone and all of them were shot down and killed. He is now remembered on the Runneymede Memorial.

Hesselyn Drive – Flight Lieutenant Ray Hesselyn OBE, DFM*

Born in Dunedin, New Zealand on 13th March 1921, Raymond Brown Hesselyn was educated at the Wataki Boys High School and then at the Oamaru and Southland Boys School. He became an apprentice machinist for the firm G. Poole & Son in Invercargill and during this time also joined the New Zealand Territorial Army, 1st Battalion Southland Regiment from 1936 till 1940, before transferring to the Royal New Zealand Air Force, where he was sent to Levin General Training School as an airman pilot under training on 24th November 1940.

He attended No.1 Elementary Flying School on 27th December and went solo on 8th January 1941; he was then sent to No.2 FTS on 9th February and whilst there he was injured in an aircraft accident on 24th April. He eventually received his pilots badge on 24th March 1941 and became a sergeant pilot.

Hesselyn then embarked for Britain on 26th May 1941 and was sent to No.61 Operational Training Unit at Heston finishing the course that September.

On 30th September, Hesselyn was posted to his first operational Squadron, No.234 flying Spitfires; here he flew sixteen operational flights. His stay with this squadron was to end in February, when he was selected to be one of the pilots that would fly the first Spitfires destined for the Island of Malta from the aircraft carrier HMS Eagle on 9th March 1942. On arrival at Malta, he joined No. 249 Squadron and on April Fools Day he recorded his first combat victories, shooting down a Messerschmitt 109 and a Junkers Ju87 dive-bomber (Stuka). With constant attacks daily from the Italian and German Air

Forces, Hesselyn and his comrades were in action constantly. In the space of four months fighting, he claimed 12 enemy aircraft destroyed, 6 damaged and 1 probable. He was awarded the Distinguished Flying Medal on 22nd May 1942 and ten days later was awarded a Bar to his DFM. His citation read:

During a period of four days operations in May 1942, this airman destroyed five enemy aircraft, bringing his victories to ten. Although fighting at great odds in the heavy raids on Malta, Flight Sergeant Hesselyn never hesitates in his efforts to destroy the enemy. His courage and devotion to duty are outstanding.

Hesselyn was commissioned as a pilot officer later that month. In mid-July, after completing his tour, he was posted back to Britain and sent as an instructor to No. 61 Operational Training Unit to pass on his valuable combat experience.

He then attended the Fighter Instructional School from 30th September till 28th October 1942, before being posted to No. 501 Squadron in Northern Ireland. He stayed with this squadron until February and was then sent to No. 277 Squadron flying Spitfires on air sea rescue patrols, joining them on 27th February 1943. He then joined 222 Squadron based at Hornchurch on 20th June as a flight commander. His score during his time with this squadron rose steadily.

On 17th August, the squadron was detailed to escort American B17 bombers as far as Antwerp. On the return leg of the journey, the squadron spotted a formation of Messerschmitt 109s and in the ensuing combat, five were destroyed. Hesselyn accounted for two of the enemy.

By 3rd October 1943, Ray Hesselyn had destroyed 18 enemy aircraft, 2 probably destroyed and 7 damaged. Unfortunately that same day, which saw him shoot down three 109s, he was then himself attacked; wounded in both legs and burned on the hands and face. He baled-out and was captured. He was sent to the hospital at Beauvais to treat his wounds, and from there, sent to Dulag Luft prisoner of war camp on 30th October 1943. He stayed there for one month before going to another camp, Stalag Luft 1 at Barth at the beginning of November. In a daring escape on 22nd January 1944, he made a bid for freedom, but was recaptured the following day. His own account of the escape recalls:

With Warrant Officer Olliver I escaped. At about 16.30 hours on that day, we hid in the roof of the camp theatre and remained there until about 19.00 hours, when we crawled through a ventilator on to the roof. We crawled along the roof and dropped to the ground near the gate leading to an adjacent compound which was emptey at the time. We avoided two patrolling sentry's and climbed over the gate, which was half way between two sentry towers fitted with searchlights. We then walked south-west across country. Iwas wearing a civilian jacket, made in the camp from a blanket and RAF trousers. I had a camp-made cloth cap. W/O Olliver was wearing RAF battledress. We had maps, money and a compass, but no identity papers. We carried chocolate, buiskits etc, in our pockets. At about 8.00 hours the next morning, we arrived in the outskirts of Velgast. We hid in a small wood until midday. We then went to the marshalling yard and were recaptured by four civilian policemen while attempting to enter it. We were taken to a nearby house and taken back to the camp at 19.00 hours. We were sentenced to fourteen days in the cells on bread and water.

Hesselyn was finally liberated from the camp by the Russians at Barth on 1st May 1945. Following his return to Britain and the end of hostilities, Ray Hesselyn was awarded the OBE for services during his time spent as a prisoner of war: This citation stated:

While a prisoner of war at Stalag Luft 1, Barth, Germany, this officer was appointed personnel officer in the camp. He completed this task in a most efficient and cheerful manner and was able to hand permanent records, including confidential reports on 1,400 aircrew, to the Air Ministry on release. These reports were largely the result of Flight Lieutent Hesselyn's own efforts.

Hesselyn remained in the service after the end of the war and held a number of appointments including commanding officer of 41 Squadron flying Meteor jets in March 1951 before being made CO of Biggin Hill Flying Wing the following month. In November 1954, he was on the staff at 83 Group Headquarters and in February 1960 was posted to Headquarters Fighter Command on administration duties. He was taken seriously ill and taken to the RAF Hospital at Uxbridge on 23rd October 1962, but tragically died there on 14th November. The cause of death was internal bleeding through the bowel over a long period, causing loss of Blood, this led to cancer of the stomach. He was aged just 42. Ray Hesselyn was buried with full military honours at the RAF section of the Hillingdon and Uxbridge Cemetery, Middlesex.

Hilary Close – Flying Officer Richard Hillary
Sign misspelt missing extra L

Richard Hope Hillary was born in Sidney, Australia on 20th April 1919, the only son of Michael and Edwyna Hillary nee Hope. His father had served in the army, but on discharge from the service had entered employment as a government official and was sent to Britain on a three year posting to Australia House in London. Richard was three years old, when he arrived in Britain. His family eventually set up home in Beaconsfield, Buckinghamshire and he began his education at the age of seven at the preparatory Hawnes School in Bedfordshire during September 1927. This was a boarding school which prepared boys for public school or entrance into the army or other armed services. From here Hillary continued to Shrewsbury School, where he became a top oarsman in the rowing team and eventually went on to Trinity College, Oxford to study history.

During his time at Trinity, he continued his love of rowing and was in the Trinity VIII and helped them retain their position as top team in 1938. His striking good looks and athletic physique made him a very popular young man with the girls. While studying at Trinity, he also became interested in flying and joined the Oxford University Air Squadron and was taught to fly.

At the outbreak of the Second World War, Hillary had already gained his air proficiency certificate and had been accepted into the Royal Air Force Volunteer Reserve and was called to full service on the day war was declared. He was then sent to No. 3 Initial Training Wing at Hastings accompanied by some of his fellow friends from university. From Hastings he progressed to No. 14 Flying Training School at RAF Kinloss in Scotland and after finishing that course was posted to No. 1 School of Army Co-operation at Old Sarum, near Salisbury, Wiltshire flying Westland Lysander aircraft.

On 23rd June 1940, Hillary was sent to No. 5 Operational Training Unit at Aston Down to convert to Spitfires, and from here he was posted to join No. 603 'City of Edinburgh' Squadron based at Dyce.

His first action of the war came when the squadron moved south to Hornchurch on the 27th August and he claimed a Messerschmitt 109 destroyed over Deal and another over Manston as damaged on 29th, but was in return shot down and crash-landed his Spitfire near Lympne, he stepped out unhurt, but shaken from his experience. His score increased by one enemy aircraft on 31st August 1940 and two more 109s destroyed, and one probably destroyed on 2nd September and one damaged on the 3rd, but this was to be his last day of fighting, when he was shot down in flames by Hauptmann Bode of II/JG26 off the coast at Margate. Hillary managed to abandon his aircraft although he had suffered horrendous burns to his hands and face. He floated down into the sea and was picked up by the Margate lifeboat and brought ashore.

He was sent to the burns unit at the Queen Victoria Hospital at East Grinstead, Surrey, where he was treated for his burns and underwent plastic surgery by the renowned surgeon Sir Archibald McIndoe. He spent the next three months undergoing many operations to rebuild his face and hands and became a member of the Guinea Pig Club.

During his recuperation, he decided to write about his experiences as a pilot flying from Hornchurch during that period and this was eventually published in June 1942 under the title of 'The Last Enemy.' It became a wartime best seller and has never been out of print since.

He finally left hospital in late 1941 and was posted to the RAF Staff College at Gerrards Cross in Buckinghamshire on a three-month course. Following this he managed to regain his flying category and was sent to No. 54 Operational Flying Unit at Charterhall, Berwickshire, where he converted on to twin-engine night-fighters; although several of his RAF colleagues had tried to persuade him from flying, he was determined to continue.

On the night of January 8th 1943, which was extremely cold, Richard Hillary and his navigator Sergeant Wilfred Fison took off from the airfield in their Bristol Blenheim V and while orbiting the airfield identification beacon, suddenly Hillary lost control of the aircraft and it spun in from 1,000 feet into the ground, killing him and

Sergeant Fison instantly. The crash was investigated and officials came to the conclusion that there had been a build-up of ice on the control ailerons, causing loss of the aircraft's control. Hillary's body was cremated at the Golders Green Crematorium and his ashes were scattered over the English Channel by his previous 603 Squadron commander George Denholm. He was 26 years old.

Hugo Gardens – Group Captain Petrus Hendrik Hugo DSO, DFC**

Born at Pampoenpoort, Cape Province, South Africa on 20th December 1917, Petrus Hugo was interested in aviation from an early age. He attended the Witswatersrand College of Aeronautical Engineering and by 1938 had left South Africa and paid his passage to come to Britain, and attend the Royal Air Force course at the Civil Flying School at Sywell in early 1939. Here he received fifty hours of preliminary flying training before he was taken into the RAF on a short service commission on 1st April 1939.

Here he received his nickname of 'Dutch' because of his Afrikaans accent and heritage; the name would stay with him throughout his service career.

He undertook further training at No.13 FTS at Drem in Scotland and at the end of the six week course; he was graded as exceptional by his tutor. On 23rd October 1939, he was sent to the No. 11 Group Fighter Pool at St. Athan in Wales and then on to No.2 Ferry Pool at Filton on 17th November. He was then posted to his first operational squadron, No. 615, who following the outbreak of war against Germany, were now based at Vitry in France. The squadron was equipped with Gloster Gladiators at this period.

Luckily, there was very little air action during the winter of 1939/40 and the squadron changed their biplanes for the up to date Hawker Hurricane aircraft. Just two days following the handover of their old aircraft, 'Dutch' Hugo went into action and claimed his first victory of the war, when he shot down a Heinkel bomber on 20th May 1940.

As the German armies advanced rapidly, overrunning all allied defences in their path, Hugo's squadron was told to pack up and make their way back home to England. The squadron members making their way back to Kenley and Croydon aerodromes. With the war in Europe lost and Britain now standing alone, against Hitler and his armies and air force, the Royal Air Force awaited the next phase of battle.

The official start of the Battle of Britain is recorded as the 10th July 1940, on 14th, 615 were in action off Dover, when a formation of Junkers Ju87 dive-bombers were spotted and attacked, Hugo was able to claim one of the enemy aircraft destroyed. As the fighting intensified, he claimed two Messerschmitt 109s on 20th July, and another 109 on 25th. He added one more that month, when he shared in the shooting down of a Heinkel floatplane on 27th.

In August, he claimed two more enemy aircraft, but was wounded in both legs whilst shooting down a Heinkel 111 over Newhaven in Sussex, his aircraft being damaged by the machine gun and cannon fire from a Messerschmitt 110. Hugo had not been badly wounded, was patched up and back into the fray, two days later.

He was in the thick of it again on 18th August 1940, when Kenley aerodrome came under attack by a force of German Ju88s. Hugo managed to get airborne with others from the squadron, but they were bounced by the enemy fighters and again his aircraft received heavy damage. He was wounded in the left leg, right cheek and jaw and left eye. He was able to crash-land his Hurricane and was quickly attended and taken to Orpington Hospital in Kent. He was still recovering from his wounds at Orpington, when the news arrived on 23rd August that he was to be awarded the Distinguished Flying Cross. The citation read:

Pilot Officer Hugo has displayed great keenness to engage the enemy on every possible occasion. During June and July 1940, he destroyed five enemy aircraft.

On recovery, Hugo re-joined his squadron at the end of September, now based at Prestwick in Scotland. They returned south and took up the role of patrolling convoys and some offensive sweeps over the Channel during the early months of 1941. No. 615 returned to operate from Kenley during September and Hugo had been promoted to flight commander. The squadron's aircraft had been updated and they were now flying Hurricane Mk IIs fitted with four cannon, which gave an extremely hard hitting fire-power.

He now led the squadron on raids across the Channel against German installations, shipping and army camps. During these attacks, his squadron was able to destroy twenty German vessels and damaged ten more. Hugo also claimed a share in destroying another Heinkel 59 floatplane on 14th October during a raid against the enemy base at Ostend in Belgium. He was awarded a Bar to his DFC on 25th November 1941 and given command of No. 41 Squadron at RAF Merston. Whilst leading this squadron he accounted for three more enemy aircraft between February and March 1942. His leadership skills were noticed and he was made Wing Leader at RAF Tangmere on 12th April. On the actual day of his appointment, he claimed a Focke-Wulf 190 fighter.

On the 27th April, he led the Wing on a sweep over the Channel and an engagement with German fighters ensued. The fighting took place between Cap Gris Nez and Dunkirk and Hugo was able to claim one Focke-Wulf probably destroyed and another damaged. But he was also on the receiving end once more, when he was hit in the left shoulder by enemy fire and his Spitfire was severely damaged. Hugo had no option but to bale-out over the Channel. Landing in the cold sea, he was fortunate that he was quickly picked up by the Air Sea Rescue and brought ashore to have his wound administered to. He was given a staff job at 11 Group Headquarters, Uxbridge; while recovering from his wound and whilst there was awarded the Distinguished Service Order on 29th May 1942.

Once fit to resume operational flying, Hugo was posted as a Wing Leader to RAF Hornchurch on 18th July and remained in this position for just over a month. During his time here he also flew from Hornchurch's satellite airfield at Fairlop leading No.81 and 154 Squadrons. Other squadrons within the Wing consisted of 64, 122 and 340 (Free French). Most of the missions during his time there, was escorting American bombers on daylight raids, but on 19th August, he took part in the biggest show of RAF fighter aircraft since the Battle of Britain, when the Allies attacked the port of Dieppe. Hugo left Hornchurch on 31st August 1942, and was appointed to lead 322 Wing based in North Africa.

It was here that he found his form again and shot down a Dornier 217, which he shared with another pilot on 12th November; over Bougie Harbour, Algeria. That month, he was able to claim four bombers and three enemy fighters destroyed.

At the end of November he was given command of the Wing and promoted to group captain. He was awarded the Croix de Guerre by the French on 15th February and a second Bar to his DFC on 16th February 1943. The citation read:

In operations in North Africa, Wing Commander Hugo has taken part in many sorties on which he has destroyed at least four enemy aircraft. He has displayed gallant leadership and great skill during an outstanding record of operational flying.

Hugo remained with 322 Wing until its disbandment in November 1944. His final tally of enemy aircraft stood at 17 and 3 shared destroyed, 2 unconfirmed destroyed, 3 probables and 7 damaged. He also received the award of the United States of America DFC on 14th November 1944.

For his next appointment, he was sent to join the Headquarters, Mediterranean Allied Air Force and was then to liaise with General Tolbukin's 2nd Ukrainian Army, fighting in Romania and Austria. He was posted back to Britain just before the war ended and was sent to the RAFs Central Fighter Establishment.

Hugo remained in the service after the end of hostilities with the rank of squadron leader, but with the acting rank of group captain. He retired from the RAF on 19th February 1950 and returned to his native Africa and took up farming near Mount Kilimanjaro in Tanganyika. He remained there until 1971, before a new government took away his farm and land, and he was expelled from that country. He made a new home in Karoo, South Africa, where he died on 6th June 1986.

Kilmartin Way–Wing Commander John Ignatius Kilmartin OBE, DFC

Born in Dundalk, Ireland on 8th July 1913, Kilmartin was the son of a forester in a family of eight children. His father died in 1921 and he was sent to Australia under a scheme known as 'Big Brother.' This was a juvenile migration scheme founded in 1924 by Sir Richard Linton and continued until 1953. When Kilmartin was old enough, he worked on a cattle station in New South Wales and remained there during the 'Great Depression' of the 1930s.

He then left Australia and moved to live with an aunt in Shanghai, China, where he got employment working as a clerk for the accounts department of the Shanghai Gas Works. He stayed with this company for two years and in his spare time also became a professional jockey. In 1936, seeing an advertisement for the Royal Air Force who were looking for applicants, he wrote off to apply to join the service. He received a reply three months later, telling him to return to Britain and he made his passage back on the Trans-Siberian railway.

After arrival back in Britain, he was sent to the civilian flying training school in Perthshire and from here was sent to No. 6 Flying Training School at Netheravon on 5th June 1937. After completion of his course and gaining his wings he was posted to his first squadron, No. 43 on 8th January 1938. He was still with this squadron on the outbreak of war, but was posted to No. 1 Squadron, now in France on 3rd November 1939. Here he was known by his colleagues as 'Killy.'

That month, flying the early two-bladed Hawker Hurricane Mk 1s, he shot down his first enemy aircraft, a Dornier 17 bomber at Menchould, which he shared with a fellow pilot. It would not be until April 1940, that he was again in action and shot down a Messerschmitt 109 on 2nd April and a Junkers Ju88 on 20th.

When the Germans launched their Blitzkrieg attack against Holland, Belgium and France on 10th May, No. 1 Squadron was again in action, with Kilmartin claiming 10 enemy aircraft over the next seven days of battle. But, the struggle was in vain and the German armies advanced to the Channel and defeated all before them. No. 1 Squadron was ordered back to England on 24th May 1940.

He was then posted to be an instructor at No. 6 OTU at Sutton Bridge, where he passed on the valuable combat experience he had gained fighting in France. He was then transferred to No. 5 OTU at Aston Down, where on 16th August, he crashed his Hurricane aircraft, but stepped out unscathed.

As the Battle of Britain was at its peak, Kilmartin was sent to No.43 Squadron at Tangmere in Sussex on 4th September, the squadron having suffered a number of casualties. Two days later, he shot down a Messerschmitt 110 and on 7th, a Me109.

The following day, the squadron was withdrawn from the fighting and sent north to Usworth. He was awarded the DFC on 8th October 1940. His citation stated the following:

Flying Officer Kilmartin has destroyed twelve enemy aircraft. His dash and determination, with clear thinking, combine to make him a magnificent leader

In April 1941, he was posted to command No. 602 'City of Glasgow' Squadron, but his command was short and a month later he was sent to RAF Catterick in Yorkshire to help form the Czechoslovakian Squadron, No. 313. Kilmartin was ordered to go to West Africa in

June 1941, and he took over command of No. 128 Squadron based at Hastings in Sierra Leone in March 1942 and remained with this unit that August. He returned to Britain and following leave was appointed as Supernumerary Squadron Leader with No.504 Squadron at Middle Wallop in Hampshire. He became the commanding officer in early March 1943.

His next move was to become Wing Leader at Hornchurch taking over from Wing Commander A. M. Bentley on 30th March 1943. Here, he had two squadrons under him, No. 122 and No. 453, an Australian squadron. At Hornchurch during this time, Kilmartin led his Spitfires on bomber escorts, mainly at high altitude. The squadrons were using Mk IXAs which had a two-stage supercharger engine, which gave a plus boost to 25,000 feet, which was almost unheard of and took them up to a level 30,000 feet, which could get them above the German fighters.

He flew numerous missions over northern Europe taking the Allied bombers as far as they could, which was the German border. Kilmartin was posted away from Hornchurch on 30th May 1943 and sent to No. 61 Operational Training Unit briefly, before going to Headquarters 84 Group as Wing Commander Operations with the newly formed 2nd Tactical Air Force.

He was then given command of 136 Wing in May 1944, and following the D-Day invasion, the squadrons were in action with their rocket-firing Hawker Typhoon aircraft causing mayhem against the Germans. The Wing was disbanded at the end of June and Kilmartin was sent back to Headquarters 2nd Tactical Air Force as Wing Commander Fighter Operations and remained in this position until the end of hostilities in Europe in May 1945.

The next month, he was posted to Burma with the war against the Japanese still raging. Here he was made Wing Leader of 910 Wing equipped with American Lockheed P47 Thunderbolt fighter aircraft. His role here ended with the Japanese surrender in August 1945.

Post-war, Kilmartin returned to the United Kingdom and remained in the RAF. He held various appointments which included time at the

Air Ministry on the staff of the Deputy Chief of Air Staff on the fighter side until 1952 and in 1957 commanded the Control and Reporting Station at Borgentreich, Germany until July 1958. Following this, he retired from the service that month.

Having married and started a family, he ran a chicken farm in Devon before retiring. John Kilmartin passed away in October 1998.

Kingaby Gardens – Wing Commander Don Kingaby DSO, DFM** DFC (US) AFC

Donald Ernest Kingaby was born on 7th January 1920 in the Borough of Islington, London, the only child of Percival and Esther Louisa (nee Hastings) Kingaby. His family moved frequently as his father pursued a living as a Church of England minister and his early childhood was spent in London, Suffolk, Hertfordshire, Ontario, Canada, and finally at Histon in Cambridgeshire.

During his time in North London, living near the gates of Highbury Stadium as a ten year old, he established a life-long love of Arsenal football team, especially as they entered their fabulous run of success which continued all through the 1930s.

In 1934, he enrolled at King's School, Ely which was a boarding school and played for the school's First XI. Upon leaving school at the age of sixteen, he went to work for the Ocean Accident and Guarantee Corporation Limited in Cambridgeshire, where he worked from 1936 to 1939. As the threat from Germany became stronger, and he was now old enough, he joined the RAF Volunteer Reserve and was accepted for training as a sergeant pilot in April 1939. After part-time training, he was called up in September as war was declared. He was then sent to No. 5 Operational Training Unit at Aston Down on 10th June 1940, where he spent a seven day, ten hour conversion course and was taught how to fly a Spitfire fighter aircraft. He was posted to his first squadron on 24th June and preceded to Wittering in Cambridgeshire to join No. 266 'Rhodesia' Squadron.

On arrival to his new squadron, Kingaby was highly elated and bursting with the overconfidence of every newly trained pilot. He then proceeded to demonstrate all the wonderful things he could do with a Spitfire! Upon landing, he was sent immediately to the squadron commander, where he was 'verbally trimmed, pruned and cut down to size' during a fifteen minute tongue lashing.

During the early weeks of August 1940, the squadron was sent south to operate from Eastchurch, as part of 11 Group, and here on 10th August the airfield came under attack. Kingaby narrowly missed death by escaping from a hut he had just slept in, which received a direct hit. He with commanding officer, Squadron Leader Rodney Wilkinson was also instrumental in saving some Spitfires in a burning hangar.

Kingaby's first success against the enemy came two days later on 12th August, when 266 was ordered to patrol over the Solent Estuary and the south of Portsmouth. At 12.05 pm, they sighted twelve German aircraft, a mixed formation of Me110s and Junkers Ju88s. Kingaby was able to attack one of the Ju88s from astern and firing at it, saw the starboard engine ignite and also pieces of the fuselage breaking off. He then turned his attention to another Ju88 and observed hits on this also and damage to its fuselage. He then noticed a Me110 heading out to sea, eventually catching up with it sixteen miles from the French coast. Again firing his guns, he saw smoke and flames billowing from both its engines. On return to Eastchurch, he put in a claim for three damaged enemy aircraft.

On 18th August, Kingaby escaped with his life once more, when just after 266 Squadron had landed from a sortie at Manston aerodrome to refuel, they came under fire from a surprise attack on the airfield by Messerschmitt 109s at low-level. The pilots on the ground ran in all directions seeking cover as the airfield defences sprang into action against the raid.

Kingaby threw himself to the ground as the enemy fighters strafed the airfield, rolling from one position to another as bullets hit the ground around him. As the last Me109 flew over, he picked himself up and ran to the nearest shelter. His only wound was a bloodied hand

and two bullet holes which had pierced his flying suit, but not his body.

The squadron was soon withdrawn from the battle and sent to Wittering to rest and take on new pilots. On 25th September, he was posted to join No. 92 Squadron at Biggin Hill, Kent. Kingaby was in action with the squadron on 27th and claimed a Me109 damaged and one other damaged on 30th. His tally of enemy aircraft began to mount through October and November with nine enemy aircraft destroyed and one damaged. Four of the enemy aircraft he shot down was in a single day on 15th November 1940.

On 6th December 1940, he was awarded the well-earned Distinguished Flying Medal awarded to non-commissioned officers. The Air Officer Commanding 11 Group stated:

On 15th November 1940, in particular, this gallant young Sergeant Pilot scored a magnificent success, personally destroying four enemy aircraft. He has shown great tenacity and has destroyed nine enemy aircraft and probably destroyed or damaged a further four. I strongly recommend him for an immediate award of the Distinguished Flying Medal.

The squadron started offensive operations over the Channel in February 1941 and Kingaby started the New Year with shooting down a Me109 in mid-Channel on 14th February.

While having an evening off and attending a dance at the Bromley Country Club during that spring, he met Helen Watkinson then aged twenty, who worked as a secretary at Robinson & Cleaver, a draper's firm from Belfast, which had premises on Regent Street in London. They started courting and fell in love.

Throughout the remainder of 1941, his score steadily increased and by 3rd October, he had added another eight Me109s destroyed, four probably destroyed and two damaged.

He was awarded a Bar to his DFM on 29th July and a second Bar on 11th November 1941. Don Kingaby was the only man to be awarded three DFMs during the war. This is now recorded in the Guinness Book of Records. On 15th November, he was commissioned as a pilot officer.

That same month, he was rested from operations and sent to No. 58 OTU at Grangemouth as an instructor. On 7th February, Kingaby and his finance Helen were married at St. John's Church in Bromley and spent their wedding night at the Waldorf Hotel. He remained as an instructor until March 1942, whereupon he was posted to No. 111 Squadron at Debden. He was there only a month, before he was sent to RAF Hornchurch to join No. 64 Squadron commanded by Squadron Leader Wilfred Duncan-Smith, another excellent fighter pilot who was extremely successful and a good leader of men.

Kingaby's first claim with his new squadron came on 2nd June, when the Hornchurch Wing consisting of 64, 122 and 313 Squadrons was detailed to act as close escort to six Hurricane fighter-bombers on Circus operation 181 that morning. Crossing the French coast at Le Crotoy, they proceeded up the Somme Estuary for about five miles, when a number of Focke-Wulf 190s approached them from head-on. Kingaby opened fire giving a one second burst as one of the Germans machines approached. He saw strikes on the fuselage and for a few seconds a stream of black smoke. He fired again, but did not see any further hits. On return to Hornchurch, he claimed the enemy aircraft as damaged.

On 30th July1942, he entered the record book again as being the first pilot to shoot down the enemy using the new Spitfire Mk IX. No. 64 Squadron had been the first unit to be equipped with the new type and had only become operational two days earlier.

In August, on 19th, the squadron took part in providing air cover for the Allied raid on Dieppe; Kingaby claimed a Dornier 217, ten miles south of Dieppe. That month, he was also made flight commander of No. 122 'Bombay' Squadron, also based at Hornchurch. In November, he took over command of the squadron and by March 1943 had added another three enemy aircraft to his score. On 24th February, he was awarded the Distinguished Service

Order and his wife had given birth to a baby son on 15th March, naming him David.

As his tour expired in May, he spent a year on a staff appointment at Fighter Command Headquarters, Bentley Priory. He returned briefly to operations during June 1944, when D-Day was launched and the Allies stepped ashore at Normandy on 6th June. At that time, he was attached to 501 Squadron and it was while with them, that he claimed his final aircraft victory of the war; a half share in a Me 109, shot down in the Cazelle area.

There then followed a posting at the Advanced Gunnery School at Catfoss, where he worked under his former Wing Leader 'Sailor' Malan. By the end of the war he had been further decorated with an American DFC and Belgium Croix de Guerre. On 21st November 1944, his wife presented him with a second son Stephen Michael.

In January 1945, he was posted abroad to India for eighteen months, in March he learnt that his baby son had tragically died of crib death and he was not granted leave. His wife was devastated and did not see her husband again until 1946. Following his demobilisation in July 1946, Kingaby re-joined the RAF and accepted a posting on the military staff assigned to Air Chief Marshal Sir Guy Garrod at the RAF Delegation to the United Nations in New York, his family following him to America in April 1947. On 24th September, his wife bore him a daughter, Patricia, Katherine, known as 'Tish.'

He returned to Britain to take up command of No. 72 Squadron in February 1949 at Odiham and then at North Weald, Essex. During this time he led the Vampire jet aerobatic team, who were the first to roll seven aircraft in line abreast. It was at North Weald, he became the proud father of a second daughter, Susan Margaret, born on 15th January 1951. On 5th June 1952, he was awarded the Air Force Cross.

His final years of service, was as Wing Commander 139 Wing at RAF Celle in Cologne, Germany. On 29th September 1958, he retired from the service retaining the rank of wing commander. In civilian life he started a new career in a company named International Prints and became manager, his job involved distribution of movies throughout

Europe for the Universal Pictures Corporation. He remained with this company until 1983, when it was discovered that he had two aneurisms in his head that required immediate surgery. The surgery and those that followed led to his full retirement.

In 1985, he and his wife decided to live in the United States, to be closer to their children and grandchildren and settled in Westfield, Massachusetts.

In late October 1990, Don Kingaby suffered a stroke, but a second more serious stroke completely paralyzed him that November. Tough and determined to the end, Don Kingaby passed away from pneumonia on New Year's Eve 1990. His wife and family brought his ashes home to England to the family plot in Bromley and a special memorial service was held at the Biggin Hill RAF Chapel on 21st September 1991. The road in Hornchurch now pays tribute to one of the greatest fighter pilots in history

Kirton Close – Sergeant Pilot David Kirton

Born in Dover on 2nd June 1919, David Ian Kirton was the second son of James and Violet Kirton. Tragically, his father who was serving in the Royal Navy as an electrical artificer 3rd Class at the shore base of HMS Tarlair in Scotland contracted pneumonia and died on 9th November 1919, leaving his expectant wife to bring up two children, the older son also named James. Living at No. 20 Marine Parade, David was educated at St. James School, Dover and then at the County School for Boys.

On leaving education in 1935, he worked as an apprentice printer for the Dover Express newspaper for a short while, but at the age of sixteen joined the Royal Air Force as his elder brother had done, as a boy entrant later that year. He was then posted to the RAF School of Photography at Farnborough, Hampshire. He applied for pilot training and was selected and began ab-initio-training at the No. 22

114

Elementary and Reserve Flying Training School in Cambridge on 12th June 1939. From there he went to No. 6 Flying Training School at Little Rissington in mid-August, and after completion of this course was sent to No. 5 Operational Training Unit at Aston Down to convert on to fighter aircraft on 23rd March 1940.

He was sent to his first operational squadron; No. 501 based at Tangmere in Sussex on 27th April, but was posted to Hornchurch on 5th May to join No. 65 Squadron. He flew operations throughout early July in many patrols in the lead up to the Battle of Britain.

On 8th August 1940, while 65 Squadron was intercepting a raid over the south-east coast, he was killed when he was shot down at 11.40 am, after being bounced by Messerschmitt 109s over Manston in Spitfire K9911, his aircraft crashing in flames at Pegwell. The Luftwaffe pilot, who shot him down was Oberleutnant Willy Fronhoefer of Jagdeschwader 26 based at Caffiers in France. David Kirton's body was recovered from the crash-site and was buried alongside his late father, with full military honours on Tuesday 13th August, following a well-attended funeral service at St. James Church, Dover. He was buried in the church's cemetery aged just 21 years.

Sadly, his older brother James, who had risen to the rank of squadron leader, was also killed while flying a Wellington bomber on a training flight on the night of 27th January 1944. He is buried in Desborough cemetery, Northamptonshire. Their mother remarried after the war and lived to the ripe old age of 96. She sponsored a wooden bench in memory of both her son's which stands in Granville Gardens, Dover. At Hawkinge in Kent, there is also a road named after David Kirton in his memory.

Leathart Close– Air Commodore James Leathart CB, DSO

James Anthony Leathart was born in Upper Norwood, South London on 15th January 1915, his father was a doctor who went on to become a distinguished surgeon in the field of ear, nose and throat; whose own father had been equally famous as an art loving industrialist in Newcastle upon Tyne in the 19th Century, who patronised the Pre-Raphaelite artist movement and had built up his own collection. James Leathart's grandmother had been painted by the famous Rossetti and her portrait hangs in the Tate Gallery.

He was educated at St. Edward's School at Oxford and from there went to Liverpool University, where he studied engineering. During this period, he joined as a founder member of No.610 (County of Chester) Royal Auxiliary Air Force Squadron, much to the annoyance of his parents, who found out that he had abandoned his degree course in favour of flying.

Base at Hooton Park, he learnt to fly on Hawker Hart aircraft and gained his wings on 2nd May 1937 and was assessed as average. He then continued his flying at No. 3 Flying Training School at Grantham until the end of July, before moving to South Cerney flying Hawker Furies. On October 26th, he was sent to the Advanced Training Squadron at Penros and on completion was given above average rating.

On 27th November 1937, he was posted to his first operational squadron, No. 54 at Hornchurch in Essex and undertook his first flight there in a Hawker Hart, doing circuits and landings on 8th December. Eight days later, he took his first flight in one of the squadrons Gloster Gladiators, the RAFs top aircraft at that time. He was given the nickname of 'Prof' by his fellow officers, because of his academic background.

James Leathart accompanied Squadron Leader Max Pearson to Eastleigh aerodrome, near Southampton on 3rd March 1939 in a Fairey Battle to pick up the first Spitfires for 54 Squadron, Leathart flying Spitfire K9980. He was promoted from pilot officer to flying officer on 1st September 1939, just two days before the outbreak of war with Germany.

His first action was over Dunkirk and on 21st May 1940, when he claimed a Heinkel 111 bomber, but this was unconfirmed. That same day, he had seen the commanding officer of 74 Squadron, also based at Hornchurch, force-land his Spitfire at Calais-Marck airfield after it was damaged in action. On return to Hornchurch, he suggested that a rescue attempt might be made to pick up Squadron Leader 'Drogo' White and bring him home. After authorization from group headquarters, the rescue attempt was launched in which Leathart would fly a two-seat Miles Master trainer escorted by two 54 Squadron Spitfires.

After flying at low-level across the Channel to Calais-Marck, Leathart landed his aircraft, while the two Spitfires circled as protection overhead. Leaping from his aircraft, he could find no sign of Squadron Leader White, so after a few minutes decided to take-off again. As he did so, suddenly he was attacked by a Messerschmitt 109, one of several flying at various heights over Calais-Marck. Leathart immediately saw tracer bullets passing his aircraft's wing and immediately slammed his aircraft down onto the ground of the airfield and jumped out and ran for the nearest ditch; as he jumped into the ditch, he found White there also taking cover. The two men watched the aerial battle going on between the Me109s and his two comrades, Alan Deere and Johnny Allen for a number of minutes, before the Germans retired. Deere and Allen had accounted for three of the enemy.

After the noise of battle had abated, Leathart and White jumped from the ditch and made their way to the Miles Master aircraft, which fortunately was not damaged. They had to hand-crank the aircraft to start the engine and on firing, took off and headed for England, again at low-level. They landed at Manston to refuel and flew back into Hornchurch at lunchtime.

Leathart led the squadron on many sorties during this period in May and claimed another six aircraft up to 27th May. For his outstanding

117

courage and leadership during the Calais-Marck rescue, he was awarded the Distinguished Service Order on 31st May 1940 and was presented with the award by His Majesty King George VI at RAF Hornchurch on 27th June. He was made a flight lieutenant in August and continued to lead 54 Squadron throughout the Battle of Britain until they were sent for a rest period to Catterick in September 1940. In the period from June to early September, he accounted for a further 5 enemy aircraft destroyed, 2 probably destroyed and 3 damaged.

On 18th November, he was posted to the Air Ministry Deputy Directorate of Air Tactics and remained there till 3rd March 1941, when he was sent to Headquarters Fighter Command on the staff of night-fighter operations. Following this, he moved on to become officer commanding No. 406 (Canadian) Night Fighter Squadron based at Acklington on 10th May 1941.

He left this appointment and was sent to Headquarters Middle East as a Wing Commander Tactics on 8th November that year. He was then given the job of commanding officer o0f No. 89 Squadron on October 16th 1942 and while flying with this unit destroyed an Italian Cant Z-1007 aircraft on the night of 22/23rd February 1943 over northern Tripoli, whilst flying a twin-engine Beaufighter aircraft.

He returned to the United Kingdom in early 1944 and joined the air staff of No. 84 Group, 2nd Tactical Air Force and then became the personal pilot for Air Chief Marshal Sir Trafford Leigh- Mallory, during the build-up of preparations for the Normandy invasion.

On 30th May 1944, Leathart volunteered to join a mobile light-Warning Radar unit which would go ashore soon after the D-Day landings. The unit consisted of Jeeps and would control night-fighter squadrons on the day of the invasion. He landed on Juno Beach at H-hour + 5. Once ashore the unit went into operation and during this time, Leathart had a hand grenade land near him, fortunately it failed to explode.

He was given command of No. 148 Squadron in March 1945, part of No. 85 Group, a four squadron wing flying Mosquito night-fighter

118

aircraft, whose role was to support the Allies advancing across Europe.

At the end of the war, he remained in the RAF and was appointed on the Directing Staff at the RAF Staff College until 7th January 1948, when he was posted as Wing Commander Ops at Headquarters 66 Group. January 1950, saw him working at the Joint Services Staff College and in August the same year he joined the RAF Member of the Joint Intelligence Staff. On 18th January 1954, he was made Wing Commander Flying of Northern Sector Fighter Command and a year later promoted to Group Captain Officer Commanding Air Defence Operations Centre Fighter Command. At the beginning of July 1957, he was posted as Station Commander, RAF North Coates which was the first RAF guided weapons station and operations research centre for air defence missiles; here he helped to introduce the new Bloodhound missile.

He achieved the rank of air commodore on 7th December 1958 and was made senior air staff officer of No. 12 Group. He was awarded the Companion of the Order of the Bath on 11th June 1960, his final post was as Director of Operational Requirements, Air Ministry, where finished his RAF service and retired at his own request on 24th July 1961. He set up home with his wife Elaine whom he had married in 1939, with their children at Wotton-under-Edge in Gloucestershire. He lived there until his death on 17th November 1998.

Locke Close – Flight Lieutenant Eric Lock DSO, DFC*
Name misspelt with extra e added

Hornchurch can proudly boast that one of its fighter pilots became the top scoring ace during the Battle of Britain; his name was Eric Stanley Lock.

Lock was born on 19th April 1919 at Bomere, Bayston Hill, near Shrewsbury in the county of Shropshire. He was the youngest son of Charles and Dora Lock nee Cornes who farmed Bomere Farm and worked the adjacent Sharpstone Quarry. Both his parents' families had been involved in farming for generations; his mother's family, originally from Cheshire, had moved southwards in the nineteenth century.

His early years were happy and he would have many adventures playing in the nearby woods, which stood at the edge of the family farm; where he would play with his sister Joan. By the age of seven, he was sent to a boarding school at Clivedon, Church Stretton that was run by a Mrs Pearson.

He moved from there to the old Shrewsbury Boy's High School and from here to Prestfelde School situated in London Road, Shrewsbury. Lock became popular with both teachers and students alike and distinguished himself in both track and field sports. Another of his pastimes was horse-riding and became a member of the Shropshire Pony Club; he also rode with the South Shropshire Hunt.

His first interest with aviation was building the 'Meccano' metal aeroplanes and at school his exercise books would often be filled with sketches of flying machines. His first encounter with an aircraft came when he was twelve years old and was given a 'five bob flight' when Alan Cobden's flying circus visited the county. Lock liked speed and eventually bought a Norton motor cycle and would speed around the country lanes.

Finishing his schooling in 1933, he helped his family farm the land and also worked driving lorries in and out of the quarry works. By the mid-thirties, Eric Lock's interest in flying had grown such that he would often take trips to Longmynd airfield to watch gliders. And it was at one of these gliding meetings that Lock would meet and talk with one of the contemporary celebrities of the air, the record breaking pilot Amy Johnson.

Lock's ambition to become an airman turned to reality, when aged eighteen he joined the RAF Volunteer Reserve in February 1939 as an Airman-under-training pilot. He undertook his part-time training at Meir, near Stoke-on-Trent, which consisted of weekend flying instruction on Tiger Moth aircraft and attending evening classes. His progress was outstanding and by 3rd March 1939, he had taken his first solo flight and was awarded his pilot's certificate in May and given the rank of sergeant pilot.

With the outbreak of war against Germany almost imminent, he was sent to join No. 41 Squadron at Catterick, North Yorkshire. During the early part of the war, its pilots saw no action and Lock was given the task of ferrying aircraft across the Channel to Abbeville in France.

In July 1940, Eric Lock married Miss Peggy Mayers, the only daughter of Mr and Mrs J.A. Mayers of London, Ontario, Canada. Peggy had been a former Miss Shrewsbury. They married at St. Julian's Church, Shrewsbury.

It was at this time that he acquired his RAF nickname of 'Sawn off,' given to him by his fellow squadron friends, because of his small dumpy stature (he was only 5ft 6ins) when wearing a Sidcot flying suit; but most of the time he was just known as 'Lockie.'

On 15th August, while operating from Catterick with 41 Squadron, Lock claimed his first enemy aircraft. When flying Spitfire R6885, he destroyed a Messerschmitt Bf 110 fighter-bomber over the Bishop Auckland area; but it would be down south in No. 11 Group Sector during the Battle of Britain that his skills would come to the fore.

Having returned with 41 Squadron to RAF Hornchurch on 3rd September 1940, two days later Lock was to achieve considerable success. At around 2.15 pm, No. 41 Squadron was ordered to patrol Maidstone. At 2.30 pm a large formation of Messerschmitt 109s was sighted at between 25 to 27,000 feet. A battle ensued between the fighters and Lock was able to climb his aircraft and gain height with the sun behind him, and get behind several 109s. He fired a short burst from his guns and saw the first aircraft dive away with smoke and glycol streaming from it. The next aircraft he fired at went into a vertical dive with flames pouring from it.

On return to Hornchurch, he claimed for two 109s one destroyed and one probably destroyed.

No sooner had the squadron been refuelled and re-armed than they were scrambled once again, with instructions to intercept another raid over Sheppey.

During this encounter, Lock shot down a Heinkel and a Dornier bomber, but he was himself attacked by an enemy fighter from below and he was wounded in the leg. As the Messerschmitt banked away, Lock was able to fire on it and it exploded in mid-air. Lock's aircraft had only suffered minor damage and on landing back at Hornchurch, he was taken away to receive medical attention for his leg wound. In the course of that day he had claimed five enemy aircraft.

The Battle of Britain raged on throughout September and October and Eric Lock continued to shoot down the enemy with great success that by the end of October he had accounted for 21 enemy aircraft destroyed, 7 probably destroyed and 1 damaged. He had become the highest scoring pilot of the battle. He was awarded the Distinguished Flying Cross on 1st October and added the award of a Bar to his DFC on 22nd October 1940.

His luck was about to run out though on 17th November 1940, when as part of a formation of twelve No. 41 Squadron Spitfires, they encountered about seventy Me109s over the Thames Estuary at 25,000 feet. During the engagement, Lock claimed two 109s destroyed, before being set upon himself by an enemy machine of JG54. He was badly wounded in the left arm and in both legs, but he managed to crash-land his Spitfire at Martlesham Heath in Suffolk. For two hours, he remained trapped in his aircraft unable to free himself due to his injuries. Luckily, he was finally rescued by two soldiers who carefully removed him from the Spitfire.

They constructed a makeshift stretcher and carried him for two miles, negotiating ditches and dykes until they were able to find further assistance, and transport him to hospital for medical attention. He was taken to Ipswich hospital and treated for his wounds and remained there for a number of weeks until he was transferred to the RAF Hospital at Halton in Buckinghamshire. He was still there in December, when on 17th, he was told he had been awarded the Distinguished Service Order. His award stated:

Pilot Officer Eric Stanley Lock has been appointed a Companion of the Distinguished Service Order in recognition of gallantry displayed in flying operations against the enemy. Pilot Officer Lock showed exceptional keenness and courage in his attacks when engaged last month with his squadron in attacking superior numbers of enemy forces. He destroyed two Messerschmitt 109s, bringing his total to at least 22. His magnificent fighting spirit and personal example have been in the highest traditions of the service.

Eric Lock was to spend the next four months in hospital undergoing fifteen operations to remove shell splinters from his body. On 1st April 1941, he attended an award ceremony at Buckingham Palace to receive from the King three medal decorations for his gallantry in the air. It was the first time that one individual had been conferred this honour in wartime. When receiving his awards the DSO, DFC and Bar, the King asked him if he would be flying again soon, to which Lock replied, that he thought he would.

On 27th June 1941, he returned to his old airfield at Hornchurch to take up duties as a flight commander of 'A' Flight 611 Squadron. He was soon flying offensive sweeps with his new squadron and started to increase his score of enemy aircraft once more claiming three Messerschmitt 109s during the month of July 1941.

On 3rd August 1941, the day dawned brightly as the Hornchurch squadrons prepared to get ready for the day's missions. 611 Squadron was to be involved in carrying out Rhubarbs. This involved a pair of aircraft hopping across the Channel to France and attacking targets of opportunity if they should arise. Lock took off from Hornchurch with Flight Lieutenant Cathels at 2.45 pm and crossed into France; Cathels would fly high and Lock would fly lower ready to attack any ground targets. Lock was heard over his radio by Cathels that he was attacking a column of German troops and that was the last message he heard.

Flight Lieutenant Cathels landed back at Hornchurch at 3.25 pm, but no sign of Eric Lock was ever seen again and he was listed as missing in action. It was presumed that after he had attacked the German convoy, he was making his way back, when he was hit by enemy ground fire and killed or badly wounded and that his Spitfire crashed into the Channel.

Eric Lock was one of the Royal Air Force's youngest and gifted aces, and he had been lost at a time when they could ill afford to sacrifice such experienced flight commanders and squadron leaders. He was aged 21 years old and is remembered on the Runnymede Memorial, Panel 29 as well at Hornchurch and recently at the Shropshire Aero Club a newly re-furbished restaurant and bar named 'The Eric Lock Bar.'

Lovell Walk – Squadron Leader Anthony Lovell DSO* DFC* DFC (US)

Anthony Desmond Joseph Lovell was born at Hatton, Ceylon in India on 9th August 1919. There is very little information regarding his early life except that his father died at the age of 35-years in 1923 and that his mother brought him back to Portrush, a small seaside town in County Antrim, Northern Ireland. After attending junior school, he was sent to be educated at St. Bedes House at Ampleforth College in North Yorkshire run by Benedictine monks.

Leaving there in 1937, he joined the Royal Air Force in October that year and was sent to Sywell for training. On 22nd January 1938, he went to No. 6 Flying Training School at Netheravon and on completion of this course and gaining his wings was posted to No. 41 Squadron at Catterick in North Yorkshire on 20th August 1938.

When war was declared in September 1939, he took part in many patrols covering convoys over the North Sea, but it would not be until May 1940 that he would see any real action against the enemy.

41 Squadron moved south to Hornchurch to fly operations during the Dunkirk operation and on 31st May, Lovell was able to claim a half share with Flight Lieutenant John Webster on a Heinkel 111 bomber and another on the following day. With the operation to recovery the Allied armies from the beaches, No. 41 Squadron returned home to Catterick. His colleagues found him a charming gentleman, but he basically kept to himself and did not join in with his fellow pilots for visits to the pubs and clubs for recreation after a hard days fighting. He was a very devout Catholic.

At the start of July, Lovell and his colleagues were still at Catterick as the momentum of the Battle of Britain began to build up down south. On 8th July, he was in combat over Scarborough and helped shoot down a Junkers Ju88. On 25th July, 41 flew down to Hornchurch again as they relieved No. 54 Squadron and began operations. During the afternoon of 28th Lovell was on patrol over Dover, when his squadron accompanied by 74 Squadron was attacked out of the sun by

125

Messerschmitt 109s. During the ensuing dog-fights, Lovell was attacked by the German ace, Major Werner Molders, commander of Jagdgeschwader 51 and Lovell was wounded in the thigh. He managed to get his damaged Spitfire back to Manston aerodrome and on landing was transported to Margate Hospital for attention.

He soon recovered and returned to active service and was able to claim further successes on 15th August, when he shot down a Messerschmitt 110 fighter-bomber and damaged another during one sortie. But he was back on the receiving end, when on 5th September he was shot down over the Thames Estuary and forced to take to his parachute, he landed safely, his Spitfire crashing at Kimberley Road, South Benfleet, Essex.

He continued flying operations throughout the next three months and by the end of November 1940, he had claimed 8 and 2 shared enemy aircraft destroyed, 2 probably destroyed and 2 damaged. Lovell was awarded the Distinguished Flying Cross on 26th November 1940 and was made a flight commander. On 4th January 1941, Tony Lovell was the subject of artist Cuthbert Orde, when he sat to have a pencil drawing sketched. Orde sketched many of the famous wartime pilots and a book was published later in the war.

During the early part of 1941, he claimed three more German aircraft before his tour of operations came to an end on 23rd May 1941; Lovell was posted as an instructor to No. 58 Operational Training Unit at Grangemouth, Falkirk, Scotland. In June, he was posted from the OTU back to Catterick to become Operations Room Controller. Here he remained until October, when he was made commander of 145 Squadron at Catterick and claimed a Junkers Ju88 north-east of Hartlepool on 16th November. In January 1942, he shot down a Junkers Ju88 off Newcastle and was awarded a Bar to his DFC on 10th February.

The squadron was posted overseas to Africa on 11th February 1942 and took up position at Helwan for operations on 30th April. He resigned from 145 Squadron on 25th May and was posted to 252

Wing at Alexandria as a controller and then moved to No. 13 Sector Operations Room.

Lovell went back flying operationally, when he was sent to the beleaguered island of Malta to join 603 Squadron, but they were soon disbanded and he instead joined 1435 Flight as their commander. The island of Malta was subject to continuous bombardment from both the Luftwaffe and Italian Air Force who hoped to starve the island into surrender. During August and October 1942, Lovell was in the thick of the aerial fighting over Malta and claimed 4 enemy aircraft destroyed and a further 4 damaged. For this outstanding devotion to duty, he was awarded a Bar to his DSO on 3rd November 1942.

He was rested again from operations, and on 9th January 1943 was promoted to acting wing commander and given a role at Fighter Control Duties, 8 Sector Operations Room in Malta. He was posted to lead the Krendi Wing on 7th March, where he commanded two squadrons, No. 229 and 249; by April 9th, he was confirmed as squadron leader and prepared for the invasion of Sicily which would take place in July. Active during the Allied operations against Sicily, Lovell was put in charge of the Safi Wing leading No.126 and 1435 Squadrons.

November 9th, saw him posted away again to Headquarters North African Coastal Air Force, but he was with them only a couple of days before being sent to 242 Group.

Promoted to wing commander flying on 5th December, he joined 322 Wing and led four squadrons 154, 232, 242 and 243 from their base at Gioia Del Colle, on the island of Corsica. From here they flew operations as escort and attacked targets of opportunity in northwest Italy and southern France. During May 1944, Lovell added to his score sheet by claiming a Focke Wulf 190, a Me109 and an Italian Fiat G55 destroyed, plus a Focke Wulf damaged. Posted away again on 14th August, he joined No. 1 Mobile Operations Room, Mediterranean Air Force where he remained until 11th November, when he was sent to 244 Wing as wing commander flying to Group Captain Hugh 'Cocky' Dundas, another well respected fighter pilot who had flown during the

Battle of Britain and with Douglas Bader's Tangmere Wing in 1941. Lovell only stayed for one month before be posted to 71 OTU, Ismailia as the chief instructor. He was awarded the American DFC (US) on the 14th November 1944.

As the war in Europe entered its final year, Tony Lovell was again awarded a Bar to his DSO medal in February 1945. After the war ended against the Nazis in May 1945, he was posted on the 23rd June to the School of Air Support, Old Sarum and it was while serving here on 17th August that tragedy struck.

Taking off from the airfield in a Communications Flight Spitfire Mk XII EN234 at 11.30 am, he proceeded to do two slow rolls, when the aircraft suddenly dived into the ground and he was killed instantly. An inquiry into the fatal crash came to the conclusion that it was a mechanical failure rather than pilot error. Squadron Leader Peter Brown who flew with Tony Lovell in 41 Squadron in 1940, believed that the aircraft's ailerons might have been reversed and that while taking off, it wouldn't matter, but as soon as you climbed, the torque of the engine would cause you to drop a wing and there would be nothing you could do to stop crashing in at such a low height.

Having flown throughout the war, Tony Lovell had clocked up the largest amount of flying hours of any operational pilot. He was killed just eight days after his 26th birthday.

Malan Square – Group Captain Adolph Gysbert Malan
DSO, DFC*

Born in Wellington, South Africa on 3rd October 1910, he was the eldest son of Willam and Evelyn Malan nee Jordon and lived at Klipvlei north-east of Wellington. Adolph was initially educated at a local farm school before attending a school at Stellenbosch, which was segregated for both English-speaking and those of Afrikaan. When the family farm failed to prove successful, the family moved back to the main town of Wellington at lived in Malherbe Street. Here the young Malan continued his education at the Boy's High School.

In 1923 aged 13, Malan decided he wished to become a sailor, which shocked his parents. He managed to persuade them of his new passion and was able to apply to become a cadet on the training ship 'General Botha,' which was birthed at Simonstown. He joined sixty other cadets on 15th February 1924 and spent the next three years studying seamanship and achieved a First Extra Certificate. He left the training ship in 1927 and travelled to Port Elizabeth to join a ship of the Union Castle Line, the 'Sandown Castle' which was headed for New York. This was to be his first trip of many that would take him to all corners of the world for the next seven years.

During this time, Malan passed his Second Mates certificate and in between voyages trained with the Royal Naval Reserve achieving the rank of Sub-Lieutenant. He still hoped to achieve more with his life and was still soul-searching, when he learnt that several of his colleagues had applied for service in the Royal Air Force in 1935. He received a letter telling him that he had been accepted, and he was granted a short service commission. Before joined the RAF, he had one final sea trip aboard the HMS 'Malaya' which was conducting training manoeuvres, then he changed services.

He arrived in Britain a few months later and began his flying training at No. 2 Elementary and Reserve Flying Training School at Filton on 6th January 1936, where he was taught to fly on De Havilland Tiger Moths and undertook 25-hours duel instruction before being giving the chance to fly solo. Here he was given his nickname of 'Sailor' and was rated by his instructors as above average as a pilot. After two weeks at Filton, Malan then was sent to the RAF Depot at Uxbridge to be properly kitted out and learn drill and etiquette becoming of an RAF officer.

From Uxbridge, he was sent to No. 3 Flying Training School at Grantham in Lincolnshire and learnt to fly on Hawker Hind and Audax biplanes. The course was lasted for nine months, by which time the pilots were expected to complete at least a 100-flying hours. There was plenty of recreational sport at the camp and Malan was a keen member of the FTS Rugby XV.

At Grantham, Malan gained another nickname 'The Admiral' to add to the other nickname he had already. During the final weeks at the flying school, he flew the RAF's most up to date fighter, the Gloster Gauntlet, but he nearly cut short his career when fly a Hawker Fury, when after becoming airborne the aircraft's engine cut out and began to nose dive. Malan managed to steepen the angle of glide and the engine fortunately started again, only feet away from disaster.

On completion of this course Malan and the other pilots waited to find out if they had been selected to go to fighter or bomber squadrons their first postings. Their names were pin on the bulletin board and Malan was delighted to find he had been selected to go to No. 74 Fighter Squadron based at RAF Hornchurch in Essex on 20th December 1936.

The squadron had only recently returned from Malta and was equipped with Hawker Demon two-seat biplanes; the commanding officer was a chap named Squadron Leader D.S 'Brookie' Brookes. On Malan's personal side, he whilst serving in the Merchant Navy, had visited Britain during his travels and had met a young girl named Lynda Fraser, when he had visited her home in Ruislip, Middlesex, after he and some naval friends had been invited back to their house. The relationship had blossomed over the years and they were very much in love. They eventually married on 2nd April 1938 at St. Martin's Church at Ruislip, Middlesex.

Over the next couple of years, Malan became a well-respected member of the squadron and rose to the rank of flying officer by July 1938. Malan was part of No. 74 Squadron's team which participated in the Sir Philip Sassoon Trophy that year. It was held at RAF Northolt in early November, and they succeeded in beating 54 and 65 Squadrons, both from Hornchurch in the preliminary round of the Fighter Attack Competition. They beat off stiff competition from other squadron rivals and won the trophy at the finals held on 25th November.

In December, news reached the squadron that the new RAF fighter aeroplane, the Supermarine Spitfire was soon going to come on line with Fighter Command squadrons. Malan and Paddy Treacy were both selected to go to RAF Duxford for a course on the new aircraft. The squadron finally received its new aircraft on 13th February 1939, when Malan and Treacy travelled to Eastchurch to collect the first Spitfires and exchanged their old Gloster Gauntlets. One pilot who joined the squadron in April 1940 was Harbourne Stephen; he recalled later his impressions of 'Sailor' Malan:

He was a complete professional in my eyes, always on the ball. He had already made a name for himself at Hornchurch and was probably the best pilot on the station and was also a remarkably good shot. When we went for target practice at Bradwell, his results with an aerial gun was always far superior to any of the other pilots.

When war was declared against Hitler's Nazi Germany on 3rd September 1939, following the invasion of Poland two days earlier, the air-raid sirens sounded through-out Britain and Malan and his fellow pilots waited for their first taste of action. This was not to come for a few days, when suddenly on the 6th September, Malan's flight were ordered to take off an investigate a unidentified aircraft plot which had been picked up by Radar over the North Sea heading in towards the north Essex coast. Hawker Hurricane aircraft from North Weald aerodrome had already been scrambled earlier, now 74 Squadron were also ordered to investigate.

Malan led his flight up over the area and suddenly in the distance sighted two aircraft in the distance. Unfortunately, the call-sign for attack was heard over the radio and two of the squadron pilots, John Freeborn and Paddy Byrne dived down on the unidentified aircraft and shot them both down, killing one of the pilots Montague Hulton-Harrop.

They returned to Hornchurch only to be greeted with the news that they had mistakenly shot down two Hurricanes from 56 Squadron from North Weald. Both Freeborn and Byrne were placed under open arrest and appeared before a court of enquiry. Fortunately, they were both acquitted and returned to the squadron to continue flying operations. John Freeborn always maintained that Malan had ordered the 'Tally Ho' signal to attack, although during the enquiry Malan who appeared for the prosecution always denied this. It was a bad start to 74 Squadron's war, but they were soon to rectify this as the war progressed.

It was not until May 1940, that Malan and the squadron really got their first action against the enemy, when they were called to provide air cover over the Dunkirk beaches for the evacuation of the retreating allied armies from the clutches of the advancing Germans. Over Dunkirk on 21st May, he scored his first victories of the war against a Junkers Ju88 bomber, a Heinkel 111 which he claimed as a probable and damaged a further Junkers 88. The very next day he shared in the destruction of a Ju88 and on 24th again shared in a Dornier 17 bomber and shot down another Heinkel. On 27th, he downed a Messerschmitt 109 fighter shared a Dornier 17 and damaged two others. For this he was awarded the Distinguished Flying Cross on 11th June 1940; the citation for his awarded read:

During May 1940, this officer has led his flight, and on certain occasions his squadron on ten offensive patrols in Northern France. He has personally shot down two enemy aircraft and probably three others. Flight Lieutenant Malan has displayed great skill and courage and relentless determination in his attacks upon the enemy.

Malan was personally presented with his DFC by His Majesty King George VI at RAF Hornchurch on 27th June 1940.

His skill and determination to attack and destroy the enemy at any time and any place was highlighted when on the night of 18th/19th June, Malan flew a night sortie to engage German raiders over Essex. He was helped by the fact that it was a bright moonlit night and managed to locate the enemy and shot down two Heinkel 111s, one crashing into the garden of the Bishop of Chelmsford's residence. For this unique feat of flying and destroying the enemy, he was awarded a Bar to his DFC. On 6th July, he was promoted in rank to that of flight lieutenant.

It was at this time that Malan began to rethink the rules of air-fighting which at that time were still based on the First World War theories of air tactics. The RAF was still flying in the old restrictive formations of three aircraft in Vic shape, while the Germans were now flying a more flexible formation of either four aircraft known as the 'finger four' or two pairs. He decided to try the new system of flying and it seemed to work. He wrote up his new rules of air fighting and managed to get them printed and sent to other squadrons for their pilots to study the following year. The 10-rules that were set out stated the following:

1. Wait until you see the whites of his eyes. Fire short burst of 1 to 2 seconds only when your sights are definitely on
2. Whilst shooting think of nothing else, brace the whole of your body, have both hands on the stick, concentrate on your ring sight.
3. Always keep a sharp lookout
4. Height gives you the initiative
5. Always turn and face the attack

6. Make your decisions promptly. It is better to act quickly even though your tactics are not the best.
7. Never fly straight and level for more than 30 seconds in the combat area.
8. When diving to attack always leave a proportion of your formation above as top guard.
9. Initiative, Aggression, Air Discipline and Teamwork are words that mean something in Air-fighting.
10. Go in quickly- Punch hard – Get out!

On 10th July 1940, the Battle of Britain began and Malan and 74 Squadron moved down to Manston from Hornchurch to prepare to encounter the threat from the Luftwaffe whose first raids would be against coastal targets and convoys sailing through the Channel.

Throughout July, Malan led 74 Squadron on numerous sorties and battled with the Luftwaffe nearly every day. He was able to claim three enemy aircraft that month and on 8th August was given command of the squadron and promoted to the rank of acting squadron leader. He was a lot older than most of the pilots under his command, being thirty years old, but he was able to pass on his experience and discipline to them.

On 11th August, the squadron was scrambled early morning as the Luftwaffe formations were picked up by Radar forming over the French coast, and 74 intercepted one of these formations over Dover at 11,000 feet. They dived to attack a formation of eight Messerschmitt 109s, who on sighting the Spitfires went into a half-roll and dived away. Malan was able to latch on to one of the enemy fighters and firing his guns from a range of 200-yards, the German again turned his machine to avoid Malan's bullets.

Malan stuck to him like glue as the German headed back across the Channel to France. Malan managed to get within 100-yards of his opponent before giving three more bursts of fire, which hit the Messerschmitt and caused it to burst into flames. The combat had taken place one mile north-west of Cap Gris Nez. Malan turned his

Spitfire and headed home claiming the enemy destroyed, although he didn't see it crash.

The squadron was ordered aloft once more that morning at 9.59 am, when they were told to patrol over Dover once more. Again there opposition was Messerschmitts. During this encounter, he claimed two Me109s as damaged. At 12.45 pm, the squadron were airborne again, this time without 'Sailor' when a convoy codenamed 'Booty' came under attack by enemy bombers with fighter escort. The squadron claimed several enemy aircraft, but suffered the loss of two pilots.

Malan led the fourth and final flight of the day at 1.55 pm, when they received orders to patrol Manston at 10,000 feet. A convoy was passing and nearing the Thames Estuary and a German formation consisting of Dornier and Stuka dive-bombers was sighted heading their way. Malan led his eight Spitfires up through cloud and sighted thirty Stuka's above with a Me109 escort. As the Germans began to dive down, Malan ordered four of his aircraft to take on the dive-bombers, while he and the remaining aircraft would engage the 109s. Malan attacked one of the fighters and firing from 100-yards sent it plummeting down in flames. He then climbed again and sighted a group of four Messerschmitts, he dived on these and managed to break them up and finished the remainder of his ammunition; he then set course for home.

At the end of the day, the squadron had claimed to have shot down 38-enemy aircraft. The day was christened as 'Sailor's August the Eleventh.' He was to receive a Bar to his DFC on 13th August 1940.

His role as squadron commander gave him extra responsibilities during this hectic time and he decided that he would designate more flying duties to his flight commanders, while he would get more work sorted out on the ground, he decided he would fly morning sorties, but would then get on with the paperwork which he had to deal with, which included writing the commiseration letters to the families of those pilots who had been killed or missing in action.

By the end of the Battle of Britain on 31st October, Malan had claimed 15- enemy aircraft destroyed and 7- damaged since the beginning of the war.

On 24th December 1940, he was awarded the Distinguished Service Order for his outstanding leadership and courage over that year, his citation stated:

This officer has commanded his squadron with outstanding success over an intensive period of air operations and by his brilliant leadership, skill and determination has contributed to the success obtained. Since early in August 1940, the squadron has destroyed at least 84 enemy aircraft and damaged many more. Squadron Leader Malan himself destroyed at least 18 hostile aircraft and possibly another six.

On March 10th 1941, 'Sailor' was appointed as one of the first Wing Leaders as Fighter Command started to go on the offensive, bringing the war back across the Channel into Northern France, Belgium and Holland against the Germans. Malan's posting was to lead the Biggin Hill Wing.

He again was outstanding in this role and increased his score of enemy destroyed until he was rested from operational flying in August 1941. He was never to fly operationally again. His final tally of enemy aircraft stood at 27 destroyed, 7 shared destroyed and 2 unconfirmed with an additional 3 probables and 16 damaged. He was the RAFs top scoring pilot at this time.

In October 1941, he was sent to the United States of America on a good will tour, where along with other representatives of both Fighter and Bomber Command, he travelled the width and breadth of America, giving lectures to the American Army Air Corps, visiting factories and was given the chance to fly American fighter and bomber aircraft.

On return to Britain several weeks later, he was posted to become commander of the Central Gunnery School at Sutton Bridge, where he remained for the whole of 1942.

On 1st January 1943, he was appointed as station commander of RAF Biggin Hill and was joined by other notable pilots such as Al Deere, Jack Charles Johnny Checketts and the French ace Rene Mouchotte. He did fly on some operations, but did not encounter the enemy. He was there on 15th May 1943, when Biggin Hill achieved its 1,000 enemy victory of the war, shot down by Jack Charles and Rene Mouchotte; a celebratory dinner was held at the Hyde Park Hotel in London a few days later to much merriment.

Malan remained at Biggin Hill until 7th October 1943; he was then posted to become commander of 19 Fighter Wing, part of the new 2nd Tactical Air Force on 1st November, which was being prepared for the proposed invasion of Europe the following year.

In March 1944, he was moved once more, this time to command No. 145 (Free French) Wing based on the south-coast at Merston; he remained with this unit throughout the invasion of Normandy on 6th June 1944, and flew that day leading a section of No. 340 Squadron, who acted as escort for aircraft towing Horsa gliders carrying troops and equipment into Normandy. Following this, he was sent to command the Advanced Gunnery School at Catfoss in July 1944 and from here he went to undertake a course at the RAF Staff College in 1945, where he remained until the end of hostilities. Following the end of the war, Malan was offered a permanent commission in the Royal Air Force, but he declined and resigned from the service on 5th April 1946 retaining the rank of group captain.

He and his family left Britain and sailed home aboard the 'Caernarvon Castle' to Cape Town, South Africa. Here he was offered employment to join the staff of Harry Oppenheimer's Diamond Trading Company in Johannesburg as his political secretary, he accepted the job, but became disillusioned with politics following the Nationalist Party's victory in 1950 and left. He returned to farming and bought a farm at Benfontein near Kimberley. But politics was never far away and he joined the 'Torch Commando,' a party set up of anti-fascist ex-servicemen under the banner names of 'Springbok Legion' and the 'War Veterans Action Committee.'

Malan became the organisations new president and its main criteria was to oppose the police state, censorship, racism, abuse of state power and other oppressive ideals of the Nationalist Party.

During one of its largest rallies, the Springbok Legion attracted 75,000 people from all walks of life and during a speech outside the City Hall in Johannesburg, Malan spoke of his ideals for which he had fought during the Second World War. He told those who had gathered 'The strength of this gathering is evidence that the men and women who fought in the last war for freedom, still cherish what they fought for. We are determined not to be denied the fruits of victory.'

For the next few years he continued his political interests, but he was beginning to feel unwell and sort medical advice from his doctor who advised him to undergo tests at a local hospital. He was told that he was suffering from the first signs of Parkinson's disease which attacks the central nervous system. The disease can attack either the brain or the body and in other cases both. In Malan's case, it was the body.

In 1959, he made his final trip to England, arriving at London airport, he was greeted by his old comrade Alan Deere accompanied by his wife Joan. Malan told Deere of his illness and that he was here to meet with a specialist, Sir Russell Baine to find out whether he could help with the disease. While he was in Britain, Malan was able to visit friends and go to theatres and shows one last time. He also paid a visit to his old squadron; No. 74 based at RAF Coltishall in Norfolk and was shown around the camp and sat in the cockpit of their latest aircraft, the Hawker Hunter.

'Sailor' Malan returned to his home in South Africa and his health final deteriorated to such a degree that within four years he had become an invalid, he finally passed away with his family beside him on 17th September 1963 aged 52.

Following his death, a special memorial service was held a month later at Biggin Hill, Kent in the famous RAF memorial chapel, which Malan had opened many years earlier. The service was attended by former wartime colleagues and his commander during 1940, Air Chief Marshal Lord Dowding. The Reverend Cecil King gave the address and spoke of Malan with these words:

He belonged to that happy band of brothers round whom our future lay in 1940. He had an invisible spirit to win at a time when we needed it.

So passed perhaps the greatest fighter pilot and leader of the Second World War who started his flying days at Hornchurch; and is still remembered within the Royal Air Force as one of its most famous airmen.

Mermagen Drive – Air Commodore Herbert Mermagen
OBE, CBE, CB, AFC

Herbert Walter Mermagen was born at Southsea, Hampshire on 1st February 1912. He was educated at Brighton College, where he excelled at sport, especially rugby. It was here that he was given the nickname 'Tubby' because of his stocky build.

He entered into the Royal Air Force on a short service commission in June 1930 and again because of his ruby talent was picked to play in the position of wing three-quarter for the RAF team and for Richmond rugby club. He learnt to fly at No. 2 Flying Training School at Digby in Lincolnshire from 12th July and soloed three weeks later flying an Avro 504K biplane with the rating of above average. He was posted to his first squadron, No. 43 based at RAF Tangmere on 23rd June 1931 and with this unit, he joined as part of their aerobatics team.

Mermagen was posted in February 1934 to the Central Flying School at Upavon to undertake a course to be a flying instructor and on completion was to become the flying instructor for the Oxford Air University Squadron in May 1935. The following month, he joined the staff at No. 6 FTS at Netheravon as an instructor. He returned to the Central Flying School to join on the staff in August 1936. In 1937, Mermagen led the RAF display team of three Avro Tutors in an inverted flying formation at the Hendon Air Pageant and a year later also displayed an individual performance for His Majesty King George VI. He was then put in charge of the Handling Flight at the Central Flying School and this position gave him the chance to try all of the new aircraft that would go into service with the RAF squadrons, which was unique.

When war was declared in September 1939, Mermagen was given command of forming No. 222 Squadron at Duxford in Cambridgeshire. They were initially equipped with the Bristol Blenheim light-bomber, but by March 1940, the squadron was to change over to Spitfires. He did this with such speed and effectiveness that he was awarded the Air Force Cross on 11th July 1940. It was during the changeover, that Mermagen met Douglas Bader in the Officer's Mess at Duxford and invited him to join the squadron as a flight commander, which Bader accepted.

His first combat success was over Dunkirk on 1st June 1940, whilst operating from Hornchurch, he destroyed a Messerschmitt 110. The squadron flew back to Kirton-in-Lindsey and on the night of 19th/20th June, he took off and intercepted a Heinkel 111 over Hull at 1.45 pm at 11,000 feet. The enemy aircraft was picked out by search-lights from the ground defences and Mermagen was able to make several attacks on the Heinkel before he had to break away. It was losing height with both engines badly damaged.

He continued to lead the squadron until he was posted away in late July and given temporary command of No. 266 Squadron at Wittering from 12th August, he was with them for five days until he was given a new role; to establish and command two new fighter stations at Speke on Merseyside and Valley in Anglesey from September 1940 to May 1941. In June that year, he was posted to the Middle East to take command of the Fighter Sector Station at Port Said in Egypt and then 259 Wing based at Cyprus; here he became the Service Training Officer at Headquarters Middle East and was only one of the few pilots who actually flew the rare Spitfire VB floatplane.

He was awarded the Order of the British Empire medal on 24th July 1941. Mermagen was promoted in rank to group captain on 1st January 1944 and returned to the United Kingdom in July that year, having been posted to the staff of Headquarters Allied Expeditionary Air Force following the Normandy invasion in June. He subsequently moved to the Supreme Headquarters Allied Expeditionary Forces at Versailles. Mermagen was awarded a CBE on 1st January 1945.

In this role, one of his important tasks was in SHAEF's Control Party, when he helped take into custody top German officers, like Admiral Karl Donitz, General Jodl, Field Marshal Keitel and Admiral Raeder, who were summoned to present themselves to senior British officers on board a ship in Flensburg Harbour following the signing of the German surrender at Luneburg Heath, near Hamburg on 4th May 1945. Mermagen was also invited to be part of the party which travelled to Berchtesgaden, when they arrested and interviewed the last top Luftwaffe General, Karl Koller. He served with this command until July 1945, before he was posted as air officer commanding British Air Command in Berlin.

He also received two more awards at the end of the war, which were the Commander Legion of Merit (US) and the Medal of Distinguished Service (USSR)

Following the war, he held a number of posts and learnt to fly the latest jet fighter aircraft. The French Government awarded Mermagen the Legion d' Honour in 1951.

In 1955, he was promoted to air commodore and was made commanding officer of RAF Ceylon, a post he held for two years before becoming Air Officer Administration RAF Transport Command from 1958-1960. He was made a CB on 11th June 1960. He then retired from the Royal Air Force and became a director for the bullion brokers Sharps Pixley whom he served for ten years. He retired to Gloucester with his wife Rosemary and two sons. Where, he became a devotee to golf. He died peacefully at home on 10th January 1998 aged 85

Mungo Park Road – Squadron Leader John Mungo-Park DFC*

The third child of Colin Archibald Mungo- Park and his wife Marion (nee Haswell) John Colin Mungo-Park was born on 25th March 1918 at Wallasey on the Wirral, Cheshire.

He had an older Sister named Alison and a brother, Geoffrey who had been born in 1915. The family name can be traced back to that of the famous Scottish explorer, who originated from Selkirk, who in 1795 set off on his first expedition to Africa and later in 1804 led a government sponsored expedition with the task of exploring the River Niger. Mungo Park did not return from Africa again, it is believed he was killed by natives on the Niger

John's father Colin, had worked for a steamship company, but at the outbreak of the First World War had enlisted and joined the 7th Battalion of the 7th Royal Sussex Regiment. He was promoted in October 1918 to lance corporal, but tragically he was killed on 24th October just two-weeks away from the signing of the armistice. John was only seven months old at the time of his father's death. Now a war widow, his mother was left to bring up three children as best she could, and did so despite the obvious hardships.

John Mungo- Park was educated at the local school and by 1930 having excelled in his education; this allowed him to go to Liverpool College, where he was boarded in 'School House.' Here he excelled not only academically, but as a fine sportsman in track events, rugby, boxing and cross-country.

He left full-time education in 1934 and the family moved to Bolton in Lancashire; here he secured a position within the firm of Holden's Mill at Astley Bridge and studied textiles. In his spare time he played for Bolton Rugby Club and joined the Sharples Tennis Club. It was while living in Bolton that his interest in aviation was awakened, when he became friends with the next door neighbour, a Mr Bird, who had gained his pilot's licence during the 1920s and now let the young

143

Mungo-Park borrow his aviation books, detailing the exploits of the aces of the First World War.

Now with a passion for flying, Mungo-Park decided he would seek a career within the Royal Air Force and applied. His wish was granted following an interview and medical examination, he entered into the RAF in June 1937 on a short service commission.

He was sent to No. 10 Flying Training School at Ternhill on 27th August 1937 and on completion of this course was posted to an Anti-Aircraft Co-Operation unit at Lee-on-Solent on attachment to the Fleet Air Arm on 26th March 1938. From there he was posted in August to the Fleet Requirements Unit to HMS 'Argus,' an aircraft carrier equipped with Fairey Swordfish biplanes.

When war was declared on 3rd September 1939, Mungo-Park was transferred back to the RAF and immediately posted to join No. 74 'Tiger' Squadron home-based at Hornchurch, but saw very little action until May 1940 over the beaches and port of Dunkirk during the evacuation of the British Expeditionary Force. He claimed his first victory on 24th May, when he shared in the shooting down a Henschel 126 German reconnaissance aeroplane, but during the engagement he was wounded slightly and received damaged to his aircraft. He was able to get back across the Channel and put down at Rochford airfield near Southend.

With the battle in Europe lost and the Nazis now occupying the majority of Europe, Britain now stood alone and waited for Hitler's next move. This would undoubtedly be in the form of an invasion of the British Isles. Before this invasion could take place, Hitler's Luftwaffe led by Reichsmarschal Herman Goring would have to clear the skies over Britain of RAF aircraft to allow the invasion fleet complete safety from air attack.

At Hornchurch in July 1940, pilots like Mungo-Park awaited the call, the Battle of Britain was about to begin. The first phase of the battle was for German attacks on convoys and coastal ports and installations and on 10th July, 74 Squadron were scrambled against one such raid. Mungo-Park claimed a Dornier 17 bomber five miles south of

Folkestone. On 11th August, he achieved even more success, when he was able to shoot down four enemy aircraft, claiming two destroyed and two probably destroyed.

He was promoted in rank to acting flight lieutenant at the start of September and led 'B' Flight. The squadron had left Hornchurch and were now flying operations from the No.12 Group airfield at Coltishall. On 11th September, 74 Squadron was scrambled as part of the five squadron wing led by Douglas Bader. That day they flew as rear high cover to the rest of the Big Wing. When over London, they encountered large formations of bombers and fighters and Mungo-Park who was leading Blue Section stated in his report for that engagement:

At 17,000 feet I sighted a formation of about thirty Ju88s; I carried out a beam attack and saw pieces falling off the bomber, which was leading the second section.
I broke away and climbed to 20,000 feet and attacked a Heinkel 111 from slightly above, setting the starboard engine on fire and saw him diving towards the ground.

He was able to claim the Heinkel destroyed and the Junkers as damaged. On 14th September, he was able to add to his score by destroying a Messerschmitt 110 twin-engine fighter, but did not go unscathed, receiving hits on his own aircraft from the German rear-gunner which damaged his air-intake, the propeller spinner and his port wing. He was able to get the Spitfire back to Coltishall and suffered no injuries to himself.

As the battle raged on into October, 74 Squadron was moved back into No. 11 Group to operate from RAF Biggin Hill on 16th October. Mungo-Park was in action on 20th, when he led his section of Spitfires in a patrol over their base after receiving instructions to orbit at 30,000 feet, this was at approximately 2.15 pm. They then were ordered by ground control to fly over the Maidstone area and soon sighted a formation of around thirty Messerschmitt 109s coming in from the south. Mungo-Park immediately instructed his pilots to attack, as the Germans were at a disadvantage in height at some 500 feet below them. Some of the Germans on seeing the RAF fighters dived away and headed home, while others climbed to gain height. Mungo-Park was able to get in behind the enemy fighters that were climbing and was able to fire at the last machine. This immediately went into a spin and he followed it down and saw the aircrafts tail section break away. He then noticed he had become a target himself and was forced to breakaway.

His score of enemy aircraft continued to climb and by 14th November 1940, stood at 9 destroyed, 5 probably destroyed and 4 damaged. For his outstanding success, he was awarded the Distinguished Flying Cross on 15th November, his citation read:

In October 1940, this officer was on patrol with his squadron at 30,000 feet when a formation of enemy aircraft was sighted. Flight Lieutenant Mungo-Park attacked a Messerschmitt 109, but had to break off the engagement as his windscreen became iced up. He cleaned this and again attacked the enemy aircraft and caused it to crash into the sea. He has personally destroyed eight hostile aircraft and has at all times displayed great courage and coolness in action.

On 30th November, Mungo-Park would enter the Biggin Hill record-book, when that morning at 8.00 am, the operations' room controller received a report that a convoy travelling through the Channel had come under attack by German dive-bombers with fighter escort. The weather that morning was not particularly good as thick morning fog was wide spread. However, two volunteers were asked to take off and fly over the convoy in support.

Both John Mungo-Park and his friend Harbourne Stephen agreed to fly the mission. They took off and found that the fog was only a few hundred feet in height before it cleared to clear skies. As the two Spitfires climbed and headed out for the coast they sighted a formation of enemy fighter aircraft, 109s, which were above them at around 34,000 feet.

Together they attacked one of the Messerschmitt's and shot it down; its pilot Unteroffizier Fritz Wagelain of 5/JG53, baled out, but his parachute had been damaged and he suffered terrible injuries on landing and died soon after.

On landing back at Biggin Hill they were greeted by the other pilots and photographers of the press, who were there to record Biggin Hill's 600th enemy aircraft destroyed. The pair were both jointly responsible for the downing of the German aircraft, although Stephen won the £35.00 lottery which had been running for the pilot who claimed the victory. The late Wing Commander Johnny Freeborn who was with 74 Squadron stated that he thought that it was more likely that Mungo-Park actually shot down the aircraft, but he was too much of a gentleman to dispute the decision. Either way, both Mungo-Park and Stephen both appeared in the national press as celebrated RAF heroes.

At the start of 1941, the RAF launched its offensive sweeps back across the Channel against the German Air Force. At the beginning of March, 'Sailor' Malan became one of Fighter Command's first new Wing Leaders and his position as squadron commander was taken up by John Mungo-Park and he would now lead the squadron.

It was during one of these sweeps on 16th June, that he led his men over the Channel and was successful in shooting down two enemy fighters south of Boulogne/Cap Gris Nez, after being attacked by six Messerschmitt's. His own aircraft was hit badly in the glycol tank and he headed for home, the Spitfires engine overheating finally seized just as he crossed the cliffs at Folkestone and made a forced landing at airfield at Hawkinge.

On the evening of 27th June, 74 Squadron was detailed to act as escort on a Circus operation for RAF bombers on a raid over northern France. They took off at 9.50 pm and were to be accompanied by two more squadrons, No. 19 and 266, but they became separated during the course of the trip over the Channel.

Suddenly they were bounced by enemy fighters from above and Mungo-Park's Spitfire was shot down crashing with its pilot near the railway station at Adinkerke, two miles from Belgium coastal town of De Panne.

Eye witness accounts later stated that a lone Spitfire was seen coming down trailing smoke and crashing. Mungo-Park's body was recovered from the wreckage and was buried at the Adinkerke Military cemetery. He was 23 years of age. On 9th July 1941, he was posthumously awarded a Bar to his DFC, and he had known of this award before his death in action. As well as the road in Hornchurch named after him, there is also another in Orpington, Kent, Mungo-Park Way.

Park Mews – Air Chief Marshal Sir Keith Park GCB, KBE, MC* DFC

Born on 15th June 1892 at Thames, a small town near Auckland on the North Island of New Zealand, Keith Rodney Park was the second son of three to James and Frances Park nee Rogers who also raised seven daughters. His father's occupation was that of sheep farmer, but he become a geologist and had earned himself a brilliant reputation also as an explorer and mountaineer, so much so that by 1889, he had been appointed director of Thames School of Mines and in 1901 had become Professor of Mining at Otago University in Dunedin which was situated in the South Island of the country, which forced the family to move home again.

Keith Park was sent to be educated at King's College in Auckland and remained there as a boarder until 1906 before moving and completing his time at the Otago Boys High School. It was here that he also enrolled into the cadet force in 1909 at the age of sixteen, showing great enthusiasm for anything military and patriotic, but he also had a great passion for the sea and would spend a lot of his spare time sailing. He was also keen on horse-riding.

On 1st June 1911, just before his nineteenth birthday, he found employment as a cadet purser with the Union Steam Ship Company in Dunedin. He worked on various vessels and his travels took him to Australia and the Pacific islands. During this period he attained the nickname of 'Skipper.'

He remained in this position until December 1914, following the outbreak of the First World War in Europe and was granted war leave to volunteer as an artilleryman and joined the 4th Howitzer Battery and was promoted to the rank of corporal on 1st February 1915 and was sent to Egypt. It was here that Park saw his first military aeroplane and became fascinated with flight.

His unit was then shipped out to take part in the Gallipoli campaign. The landings against the Turkish army at Gallipoli had taken place on 25th April 1915, but once ashore the Allies had met with fierce resistance from the Turks and very little headway had been made from the beachhead and both sides dug in for a prolonged trench campaign.

During the next several months Park was involved in many actions and was recognised for his achievements under fire; he was commissioned as a 2nd Lieutenant that July and was involved in the landings at Sulva Bay, where he led his eighteen pounder battery covering the Australian and New Zealand forces. He and his men came under a withering attack by machine gun fire and they only managed to fire off several rounds before seeking shelter. The sights and sounds and horrors of Gallipoli were something he never forgot.

In August 1915, Park decided he would try and become a regular officer within the British Army and he transferred to the Royal Horse Field Artillery as temporary 2nd Lieutenant on 1st September 1915 attached to the 29th Division. He remained with them until the failure of the campaign brought about the evacuation of the Allies from the Gallipoli Peninsula in January 1916. Six months after this, his division was sent to France for the beginning of the Somme Offensive arriving at the port of Marseille on 17th February, and from there they headed for their new home on the front line at Vauchelles.

149

During the journey through thick mud, Park was thrown from his horse and was injured when the animal fell on him. He was taken to hospital and stayed there for four days before returning to his unit, still unable to walk properly. When he had recovered enough, he was given the chance to accompany a Royal Flying Corps pilot on a reconnaissance flight over their own positions following a previous enemy attack that had pinpointed them from the air. Park's report stated that their own gun positions were too easy to pick out and that they needed to be better camouflaged.

On 21st October 1916, Park was wounded while trying to withdraw his guns for repair, when a German shell exploded under his horse, killing it and wounding him. He was taken to the nearest casualty clearing station and attended to and then was sent back to England to recover. He was medically certified unfit for active service and whilst recuperating was given a role as an instructor at the Artillery Depot at Woolwich. At this time, he had written off to the powers that be for a transfer to the Royal Flying Corps.

His wish was granted and on 9th December 1916, Park entered into the RFC and was sent to undertake a course of instruction at the School of Military Aeronautics at Reading, which he would have to pass if he wished to become a flyer. On passing the test, he went to Netheravon, where he was taught to fly on a Avro 504K biplane and went solo after only two and half hours in a Maurice Farman. During this flight the aircraft's throttle froze and he had to make a landing without power.

After getting a number of flying hours under his belt, Park was made a flying instructor and trained other men at Rendcomb near Cirencester. In June 1917, with 135-hours of flying in his log-book, he was posted to France to join No. 48 Squadron based at Le Bellevue, which was located between the towns of Doullens and Arras and he arrived there on 7th July. Within a week, they had moved back to a Frontier Aerodrome east of Dunkirk. Park would be flying the new Bristol two-seat fighter.

He was soon flying in action against the highly skilled German fighter Jastas, but achieved considerable success against them, especially on the day of 17th August 1917, when he accounted for four enemy machines with his observer-gunner Arthur Noss. For this action, Park and Noss were awarded the Military Cross, Park being promoted to the rank of temporary captain on 11th September. By the 15th September, he and his colleague had destroyed seven enemy aircraft and damaged five others. In December, he was sent back to Britain for a period of leave from flying and remained there until April 1918, when he received the news that he had been given command of No. 48 Squadron.

His leadership skills were exemplary, he was a tough and disciplined leader and had great understanding of the pressure that pilots could suffer through continuous flying; he was also a good tactician. At the end of the war in November 1918, Park had been awarded a Bar to his Military Cross and had also been decorated with a Distinguished Flying Cross and a French Croix de Guerre.

Park was back in England by 25th November 1918 and married a young lady he had met while in London during 1917, the socialite Dorothy Margarita Parish, known as 'Dol.' They married at Christ Church, Lancaster Gate. He was eager to remain in the service and applied for a permanent commission in June 1918, but he received no reply and applied again. He even applied for work as an instructor for the Canterbury Aviation Company back in his native New Zealand, but nothing came of this. Finally, he was awarded a commission with the rank of flight lieutenant in the Royal Air Force in 1919 and served as a flight commander with No.25 Squadron at Hawkinge. He then was posted in 1920 to take up duties as a squadron commander at the School of Technical Training at Manston, Kent and in 1922 was selected to attend the newly formed RAF Staff College at Andover.

Following completion of this course in January 1923, Park was posted overseas to Egypt and he remained there until 1925. On his return to Britain he was sent to RAF Uxbridge and put in charge of Operations, Intelligence, Mobilization and Combined Training. In

November 1927, he was awarded his next posting, that of a squadron commander and was sent to RAF Duxford in Cambridgeshire to command No. 111 Squadron, which was equipped with Armstrong Whitworth Siskin Mk IIIA biplanes. It was while here that Park escaped with his life, when he crashed his aircraft at night, landing too fast and striking a ridge, turning the biplane over. He only suffered bruises and cuts, but the aircraft was a write-off.

In April 1928, Park and 111 Squadron was transferred from Duxford and moved to the newly opened RAF Hornchurch aerodrome in Essex in April 1928. While here Park inaugurated a new working schedule; day-flying was only done during mornings and afternoons was spent servicing the aircraft and preparing them ready for night-flights in co-operation with anti-aircraft batteries and searchlights. His role was in fact as Hornchurch's first station commander.

During May, the squadron prepared to take part in the Philip Sassoon Trophy Competition which was held between fighter squadrons from various RAF Stations. The squadrons competed in qualifying heats until the final was held at Hornchurch on 24th May, No. 111 winning the trophy.

On 28th June 1928, Park played host to the famous General Balbo of the Italian Air Force, he had arrived in Britain with ten aircraft, having flown non-stop from Italy to attend the Hendon Air Pageant; Park's squadron had escorted Balbo's biplanes as they crossed the English coast and landed at Hornchurch. Park flew in the air pageant in the final display, in a mock attack by enemy bombers, his four aircraft from 111, were to intercept the raiders, which they did too much applause. Throughout the summer months, the squadron conducted air exercises and displays throughout the country.

Keith Park was promoted to the rank of wing commander on 1st January 1929, but sadly in March his time at Hornchurch came to an end, when he was posted away from 111 Squadron and sent to Headquarters Fighting Area at RAF Uxbridge, where his new job was to organise flying programmes for the Hendon Pageants. He looked back at his time spent at Hornchurch as one of the happiest periods of his career.

In January 1931, he was made station commander at RAF Northolt, but he only held this post until August 1932. Park held a number of various appointments within the RAF and had risen to the rank of group captain. His next position came in July 1938, when he was recommended by the Chief of Air Staff, Sir Cyril Newall that he be promoted to air commodore and Senior Air Staff Officer at RAF Fighter Command to Air Chief Marshal Sir Hugh Dowding.

Over the next two years, Park worked tirelessly with Dowding to improve the air-defence system of Great Britain; in Germany the threat of Adolf Hitler's growing power became more apparent that another war was looming. He was promoted to air vice-marshal and given command of No. 11 Group Sector RAF Fighter Command, which covered the area of London and the south-east of England.

In May 1940, he organised much of the patrols that flew cover over the Dunkirk beaches during the retreat from France and during the Battle of Britain, his squadrons were the main defence against the mass attacks from the German Luftwaffe between July and October 1940. Park's tactics of sending off single or pairs of squadrons to attack the enemy seemed to be the best method of causing the most damage, with the help of good communication from radar and ground control.

During this period, he would often be seen at his fighter aerodromes, arriving in his own Hawker Hurricane aircraft and dressed in a white flying suit and helmet. While there, he would obtain vital information from his pilots, in regards to the enemy tactics and any requirements that they needed. He became a very popular commander amongst his men.

But, he was however, not popular with other commanders especially those in No. 12 Group under the leadership of Air Vice-Marshal Trafford Leigh-Mallory who covered the area of the Midlands and felt left out of the battle and was left to cover 11 Group airfields in defence against enemy raids. Leigh-Mallory favoured the use of the

'Big Wing' strategy which had been instigated by one of his own squadron commanders, Douglas Bader. Their theory was attack the enemy on mass, using five squadrons in Wing formation. This theory was subject to much debate and is still being talked about today. Park's objection was that it took too long to organise five squadrons and get them in position to attack an incoming raid and that by the time they had, the enemy had probably already reached the target and dropped its bombs and was heading back across the Channel for home.

On September 15th 1940, Park was in his operations room at Uxbridge, when he had an unexpected visitor; Prime Minister Winston Churchill had arrived to view the day's operations against the Luftwaffe. This day was to be the height of the battle and when Churchill turned to Park to ask him 'what reserves do you have' Park replied 'we have none Prime Minister.' All of his squadrons had been ordered into battle.

The quarrelling between Park and Leigh-Mallory became political and those who had wanted Dowding and Park removed from their positions queued up to attack them on their use of tactics. Towards the end of the Battle of Britain, in October 1940 and Hitler's postponement of the invasion of England; both Dowding and Park attended a meeting held by the Chiefs of Air Staff and the Secretary of State for Air, Sir Archibald Sinclair and following this meeting both Dowding and Park were relieved of their commands. Park was posted to No. 23 Flying Training Command at South Cerney, Gloucestershire, while Dowding was sent to America. Strangely, Park was made a Companion of the Most Honourable Order of the Bath (CB) and attended Buckingham Palace to be awarded the medal by King George VI on 4th December 1940.

In January 1942, Park was posted out to Egypt as air officer commanding, to build up their defences around the Nile Delta. In July, as Malta became besieged and became the heaviest bombed place on earth, as German and Italian aircraft attacked the island in the hope of forcing its surrender, Keith Park was sent to command its vital air defences.

As the tide turned in favour of the Allies and Malta received more Spitfires and Hurricanes to fend off the attacks, and vital convoys arrived with food, fuel and ammunition, Malta turned from defence to offensive operations against the Germans, cutting their vital supplies to Rommel's Africa Corps in North Africa.

Park was also involved in the Sicilian campaign and by January 1944, he was made Air Officer Commander–in–Chief, Middle East Command. In February 1945, he was appointed Allied Air Commander of South East Asia and he remained in this position until war's end.

He finally retired from the Royal Air Force in 1946 with the rank of air chief-marshal and returned with his family to live in New Zealand and was later elected to the Auckland City Council. He died at the age of 82 years on 6th February 1975. On 15th September 2010, a permanent brass memorial statue of Sir Keith Park was installed at Waterloo Place in London during the 70th Anniversary of the Battle of Britain. Many of the veterans of the battle attended the opening ceremony to pay homage to their leader.

The Chief of Air Staff Sir Stephen Dalton in his speech stated that 'Keith Park was the man without whom the history of the Battle of Britain could have been disastrously different. He was a man who never failed at any task he was given.'

Pease Close – Flying Officer Arthur Peter Pease

Born on 15th February 1918 in London, Arthur Peter Pease was the eldest son of Sir Richard and Lady Pease who lived at Prior's House, Richmond in Yorkshire.

He preferred to be called Peter and was educated at Eton School from 1931 to 1936. Here he was recognised as a talented pupil and was gifted with an outstanding treble voice and was recorded singing 'O for the wings of a dove.' He was also instrumental in editing the school magazine.

He then progressed to Trinity College, Cambridge, where he studied history. It was here that he joined the University Air Squadron and learnt to fly at Marshall's Flying School. He applied for a commission in the Royal Air Force Volunteer Reserve and this was granted in September 1938. He was undertaking his final year at Trinity, when he was called up for active service in October 1939 and was sent to No.1 Initial Training Wing at Jesus College, Cambridge, after which he continued training at No. 22 Elementary & Reserve Flying Training School at Cambridge.

After completion of this course, he was sent to the No.1 School of Army Co-Operation at Old Sarum and here he met Richard Hillary and they became good friends. Hillary who later wrote his own book 'The Last Enemy' whilst recovering from burns and injuries he had suffered after being shot down in September 1940, described his friend.'

Peter was, I think, the best looking man I have ever seen. He stood six foot three and was of deceptive slightness, for he weighed close on thirteen stone. He had an outward reserve which protected him from any surface friendships, but for those who troubled to get to know him, it was apparent that this reserve masked a deep shyness and a profound integrity of character.

It was at this period that he also met Denise Maxwell-Woosnam, when attending a night skating party. They quickly fell in love and they were soon engaged.

Pease was sent to No. 5 Operational Training Unit at Aston Down on 23rd June 1940 to convert to Spitfire aircraft and on 6th July he received notice to join 'B' Flight of 603 'City of Edinburgh' Squadron based at Dyce in Scotland. His first combat experience came on 30th July, when as part of Green Section, he took off from Montrose at 11.45 am and with two other Spitfires intercepted a Heinkel 111 bomber and fired their machine guns, causing the bomber to crash into the sea. Pease was able to claim a third of a kill.

On 27th August, the squadron moved south to Hornchurch to begin front-line combat operations in No. 11 Group. Pease's next success came on the morning of 3rd September, when his squadron were given orders to patrol over Manston in Kent. When at 20,000 feet, they sighted an enemy formation consisting of six Dornier bombers with an escort of twelve Me109s and a further twelve 109s in formation above these. 603 Squadron attacked the enemy fighters and Pease was able to attack one of the Messerschmitt's and shoot it down 20-miles east of Margate at 12,000 feet. His victim was Leutnant Eckardt Roch of II/JG26 who was reported later as killed in action.

Pease like many of the young pilots, was constantly in action as the fighting in the skies over the south-east of England intensified. On 7th September, he was in action over south London during late afternoon, when following combat with enemy fighters, on his return to Hornchurch, he found that his undercarriage had been damaged and would not lower. He was forced to carry out a belly-landing back at base, which he did successfully without injury to himself. Although his Spitfire was damaged on landing, it was repairable.

Peter Pease's last combat took place on 15th September 1940, now heralded as Battle of Britain Day by the nation.

During that afternoon, 603 Squadron was scrambled for a second time, after a large raid was picked up by Radar as it assembled just over the French coast heading for the Kent coast between Dover and

Hastings, the enemy formation consisted of up to 250-aircraft. When at 21,000 feet and ten miles south-east of Chatham, they sighted 200-Me109s and Me110s at 18,000 feet below them and below these was a formation of Heinkel and Dornier bombers. They attacked the German fighters first and fought their way through to the bombers, who by this time had reached their targets in East London and were now making the return trip home. Every time the RAF fighters had tried to engage the bombers, their fighter escort had driven off any attempt to do so.

One Spitfire was able to get through the defence and began a head-on attack on one of the Heinkel bombers, but this aircraft was in turn attacked by Messerschmitts and was quickly shot down south-east of Maidstone just after 3.00 pm. The pilot had been Flying Officer Peter Pease. Years later, a German crewman Leutnant Roderich Cescotti who had witnessed the lone attacker gave an account of the brave RAF pilots last moments.

I saw a Spitfire dive steeply through our escort, level out and close rapidly on our formation. It opened fire, from ahead and to the right, and its tracers streaked towards us. At that moment a Me109, which we had not seen before, appeared behind the Spitfire and we saw its rounds striking the Spitfires tail. The Tommy continued his attack, coming straight for us and his rounds slashed into our aircraft. We could not return fire for fear of hitting the Messerschmitt. I put my left arm across my face to protect it from the Plexiglass splinters flying around the cockpit, holding the controls with my right hand. At the last moment the Spitfire pulled up and passed very close over the top of us. Then rolled over onto its back, as though out of control and went down steeply, trailing black smoke. Waggling its wings, the Messerschmitt swept past us and curved in for another attack. The action only lasted seconds, but it demonstrated the determination and bravery with which the Tommies were fighting over their own country.

Peter Pease's Spitfire continued its fall from the sky and crashed with him still aboard into the ground at Kingswood, near Chartway Street, south-east of Maidstone at 15.07 pm.

His body was removed from the wreckage and laid in a nearby shed until the arrival of the undertakers. Pease's body was eventually returned to his home and buried in the family plot at St Michael and All Angels Church at Middleton Tyas. He was just 22 years old.

Robinson Close – Captain William Leefe Robinson VC

Born in Coorg, India on 14th July 1895, William Leefe Robinson was the youngest son of Horace Robinson and his wife Elizabeth Leefe who in all had four daughters and three sons. His parents ran a coffee plantation on the Kaima Betta Estate at Pollibetta in South Coorg. As a young boy he started his education at the Bishop Cotton Boy's School in Bangalore in 1903 and on returning to England went to Dragon School at Oxford, before he later attended St. Bees School situated on the coast of Cumberland, now Cumbria in September 1909.

His elder brother Harold also attended St Bees and he took over as Head of Eaglesfield House in 1913. William was a very talented rugby player and played in the school 1st XV team. The school also had its own Officer Training Corps which William Robinson joined and they held summer camps and undertook military exercises at Mytchett near Kent; he became a sergeant within the unit.

Following the assignation on 28th June 1914 of Archduke Franz Ferdinand and his wife Sophie who were heirs to the Austro-Hungarian Empire in Sarajevo, events across Europe became increasingly stressful between nations and by that August, war loomed. On 4th August, war was declared against the Kaiser's Germany by Britain and France.

William Leefe-Robinson like many others rallied to the call and on 14th August entered the Royal Military College at Sandhurst to train as an officer. He was there for five months and on completion of his training course was given a commission as a 2nd Lieutenant to join the Worcester Regiment and posted to the 5th Militia Battalion at Fort Tregantle in Cornwall. He remained with this unit, but as it was home-based and was not sent to France, Robinson became frustrated and applied for transfer to the Royal Flying Corps and this was granted, he was posted to No. 4 Squadron based at St. Omer in France as an observer on 29th March 1915.

He was soon in action over the front lines and reporting the movements of the German forces. On 8th May, he undertook a reconnaissance patrol in the afternoon over Lille and during the flight an anti-aircraft shell exploded very close to his aircraft, his pilot was unhurt, but Robinson was wounded in his right forearm by shrapnel and began to bleed heavily, the patrol was curtailed and they returned to the airfield at Bailleul, where Robinson was quickly sent to No. 7 Station Hospital and had two pieces of shrapnel removed. He was then given one month's leave and returned to England.

After convalescence, Robinson was posted to South Farnborough on 29th June 1915 to commence flying training and become a pilot. He was there for a few weeks before going to the Central Flying School at Upavon in Wiltshire and it was here that he flew solo on 15th August. After completing his training, Robinson joined No. 19 Squadron at Castle Bromwich, Birmingham that December. He was only with this unit briefly before he was posted to No. 39 (Home Defence) Squadron based at Sutton's Farm Airfield, Hornchurch in early 1916 with the rank of 2nd Lieutenant. The airfield consisted of basic facilities, including wooden hangars and huts; most of the pilots were billeted out at homes or at the White Hart pub in Hornchurch village.

The squadron was tasked with the interception of the German airships known as Zeppelins which were now bombing towns and cities during night raids over southern England up as far as London and East Anglia. Robinson flew several patrols during the spring and summer months, but encountered his first Zeppelin on the night of 26th April 1916, he managed to climb to a height of 8,000 feet and positioned himself beneath the giant craft and fired into it, but this had little effect as the Zeppelin was at least 2,000 feet higher. Robinson lost sight of the Zeppelin as it climbed away and made its escape in an easterly direction heading back out across the North Sea.

His luck was to change however, when on the night of 2nd/3rd September, Robinson was alerted to a Zeppelin raid and given instructions to patrol between Hornchurch and Joyce Green in Kent, far in the distance search-lights had picked up a German airship over the North London area and Robinson in his BE2c biplane headed towards the illuminated enemy. The German machine was a Shutte-Lanz airship which was of wooden frame design, unlike the usual Zeppelins which were of duralumin metal.

Robinson made his attack at a height of 11,500 feet and closed within a range of 500-feet before firing off all his ammunition from his Lewis Gun, he made another approach on the target after changing his empty ammunition drum for a full one and attacked once more, but saw no visible effect. He was about to carry out his third attempt, when the airship suddenly erupted in flames and began to fall from the sky. It crashed to earth in a field at Cuffley in Hertfordshire, behind the Plough Inn; all the crew aboard perished.

The scene was witnessed by thousands of people within London and the surrounding areas; they cheered and sang as the airship descended in flames. It was the first success over the enemy raiders that had been achieved over British soil.

On landing back at Sutton's Farm, Robinson was exhausted and wished only to return to his bunk and sleep. The next morning he was transported to the scene of the crash and inspected the remains of the giant airship. He was now hailed a national hero and was awarded the Victoria Cross by King George V at Windsor Castle, where huge crowds attended to get a glimpse of their hero. He was also presented with £3,500 in prize money and given a Prince Henry Vauxhall motor car. The people of Hornchurch were so proud of his achievement that they organised a special donation fund to have a silver trophy cup made and presented to him. Thousands of postcards depicting

Robinson and the shooting down of the airship were printed and bought by the public as souvenirs, and actual pieces of the airship were sold to raise funds for the Red Cross.

He remained with the squadron for a few months, but was posted to France as a flight commander with No. 48 Squadron in March 1917, flying the new Bristol F2 fighter. On 4th April, he led a flight of six aircraft on a reconnaissance patrol around the Douai area and when they arrived, they were attacked by German aircraft of Jasta II, the famous squadron led by Manfred von Richthofen and combat was engaged.

Unfortunately for Robinson and his observer Lieutenant Edward Warburton, their aircraft was badly damaged when they were attacked by an Albatross aircraft flown by Sergeant Sebastian Festner and they were shot down. For several weeks the fate of Robinson and his colleague was unknown and they were listed as missing in action. It was not until 25th April, that news arrived that he and Warburton was still alive and in German hands. He was sent to the prisoner of war camp at Freiburg and during September 1917, together with several other officers, escaped through a window of one of the prison wings; but were captured again almost immediately.

He made another four escape attempts before being sent to the camp at Clausthal in the Harz Mountains, before finally going to Holzminden in July 1918, where he was treated badly by the camp commandant Heinrich Niemayer who singled him out for ceaseless and methodical persecution.

At war's end in November 1918, Robinson returned to Britain in very poor health following the months of harsh treatment by his captors. In December 1918, Britain and most of Europe was hit by a Spanish Flu pandemic and Robinson already weakened, became a victim of the illness. He was staying at the home of friends Nancy and Edward Clifton, when he passed away on 31st December 1918 aged 24. He was given a full military funeral and hundreds of people turned out to pay their last respects. He was buried at All Saints' Churchyard in Harrow Weald. A memorial was later erected to Robinson at the site where the airship crashed as a fitting tribute to a gallant airman.

Ryder Gardens – Group Captain Norman Ryder CBE, DFC*

Born in Risalpur, India on 28th November 1914, Edgar Norman Ryder spent his early life there until at the age of ten, he returned to be educated in England. He preferred to be known by his second name of Norman and joined the Royal Fusiliers at Hounslow in 1931, he served with them until 1934; then left the army and became a teacher at Tredennick School in Worcester, where he taught mathematics until August 1936; where after he enrolled into the Royal Air Force and was granted a short service commission. Ryder was sent to No. 9 Flying Training School at Thornby to begin his flying training on 31st October, and on finishing the course and gaining his wings was posted to No. 41 Squadron based at RAF Catterick in North Yorkshire on 30th June 1937.

At the outbreak of the Second World War, he was still with this squadron and flew patrols in protection of convoys over the North Sea during this period. Very little in the way of enemy action took place during the first few months of 1940 until, on the 3rd April, Ryder was ordered to take-off and investigate an unidentified aircraft near Whitby.

The weather that day was not very good, with low cloud and bad visibility; however he managed to locate the aircraft, which turned out to be a German Heinkel 111 on a reconnaissance mission and he attacked it and shot it down into the sea. During the attack his own Spitfire was damaged and he was obliged to ditch into the sea; on hitting the water his aircraft began to sink immediately, taking Ryder down with it to the murky deep. At a considerable depth, he managed to break free from his cockpit and with bursting lungs watched as the water turned from dark green to lighter green until he reached the surface. He gasped the air on reaching the surface and was luckily picked up by a passing trawler. For this action he was awarded the Distinguished Flying Cross on 18th April 1940.

No. 41 Squadron moved south to Hornchurch to begin operations over Dunkirk on 28th May 1940 and flew a number of sorties in protection over the beaches as the Allied troops were evacuated back across the Channel. The pilots did score a number of victories, but Ryder did not claim any enemy aircraft during this period.

He returned back to Catterick at the end of 'Operation Dynamo' and it was not until August, when the squadron returned once more to Hornchurch to relieve No. 54 Squadron that he added to his score. He claimed a Junkers Ju88 bomber as probably destroyed on 15th August, shot down six miles north-west of Seaham Harbour.

As the Battle of Britain continued into September, Ryder claimed two Messerschmitt 109s on 5th September over the Maidstone and Sheppey area, another 109 on 6th at Eastchurch and the next day a Dornier 17 bomber damaged and a 109 fighter 10 miles south of Whitstable, Kent. On 9th September, he was promoted to flight lieutenant and on some sorties led the squadron into action.

Between the 9th September to 15th, he accounted for a further three aircraft, but was himself shot down by a Messerschmitt 109 on 27th September during a squadron patrol over Kent. He baled-out and landed uninjured by parachute; his Spitfire crashed and burnt-out at East Malling. Back in action throughout October, he destroyed an Me109 on 25th October and two more on 30th. His final victory came on 27th November, when he destroyed an Me109 over Ashford.

During January 1941, Ryder was appointed commander of No. 56 Squadron at North Weald and led it on the first of many offensive operational sweeps over the Channel into Northern France during that spring. In June, he was posted to lead the Kenley Wing and was awarded a Bar to his DFC medal on 29th July 1941.

On 31st October, he was leading the Wing as protection for a low-level enemy shipping strike by Hawker Hurricanes, when his aircraft was hit by anti-aircraft fire and he was forced to bale-out over enemy territory. He was captured by the Germans and sent to a prisoner of war camp, where he escaped in 1943 and managed to reach Poland before being recaptured and sent back to spend the rest of the war in captivity. Finally repatriated in May 1945, he was awarded a Mention in Despatches for his distinguished service while as a prisoner of war on 28th December 1945.

In peacetime, he remained in service with the Royal Air Force and was awarded the Order of Orange-Nassau and also the CBE on 1st January 1958. On 11th August that year, he was given the appointment of Station Commander at RAF Duxford, Cambridgeshire and took part in the London to Paris Air Race Competition held in 1959, before finally retiring from the service on 28th October 1960 as a group captain. In later years he moved to Arizona in the United States and died there in 1995

Sarre Avenue – Sergeant Alfred Richard Sarre

Very little known about Alfred Sarre's early life, but was always known as 'Joey' Sarre by his RAF colleagues. He joined the RAF Volunteer Reserve in March 1939 as an airman-under-training pilot (serial number 745543) and was called up two days before the outbreak of war on 1st September 1939 and was sent to No. 15 Flying Training School at Lossiemouth in Scotland, here he began his flying training on No. 6 Course of the Initial Flying School on 2nd January 1940. Having completed this course on 18th March, Sarre moved to the Advanced Training School and left there on 8th June 1940. Two days later, he was sent to No. 5 Operational Training Unit at Aston Down to do conversion training on to Spitfire aircraft.

Having obtained around 20-hours flying time, Sarre was posted to No. 263 Squadron based at Drem, Scotland on 23rd June and while there flew Hawker Hurricanes. Within days, the squadron had moved to Grangemouth and soon were to receive new aircraft, the twin-engine Westland Whirlwind fighter. The pilots were offered the choice of converting to the new type or remain on single-engine fighter aircraft. Sarre chose the latter and was posted away to join No. 603 Squadron at Dyce on 3rd July; the squadron was equipped with Spitfires.

It was not until the squadron moved to Hornchurch in Essex on 27th August 1940, that 'Joey' Sarre saw his first action of the war as the enemy raids intensified. On Friday 30th August, 603 Squadron were scrambled and six Spitfires took off at 10.35 am to intercept a large formation of Messerschmitt 110s escorting bombers and were sighted over Deal in Kent. Sarre and his fellow pilots went into attack and scored several hits on the enemy; Sarre himself did not account for any of the enemy aircraft, but did receive damage to his own aircraft with bullets in the tail section. He was in action again during the afternoon, when they encountered another incoming raid over Canterbury.

Sarre was able to claim a Messerschmitt 109 as a probable, but in turn was shot down at 4.55 pm. The tail of his Spitfire was shot away and he was forced to take to his parachute. His combat report of the action read:

When on patrol with 603 Squadron at 25,000 feet, we sighted enemy formation at 20,000 feet, with enemy fighters above them. I became detached from the squadron and was attacked by a formation of four Me109s from the starboard quarter. I turned into them and opened fire. I was unable to see the result of my fire, as my machine fell into a violent spin. On landing by parachute I was met by Flying Officer Delg of West Malling, who had witnessed the combat through field glasses, and said he had seen one Me109 fall away and enter into a steep dive, but had not watched the enemy aircraft crash.

On Wednesday 4th September, Sarre was one of twelve pilots from 603 that took off from Hornchurch at 12.45 pm and ordered to patrol Gravesend and following this were given instructions to patrol Manston. Sarre along with Ken MacDonald became separated from the rest of the squadron and when at 30,000 feet sighted six enemy fighters, 4000 feet below them. Sarre and his comrade dived to attack and fired their machine guns, MacDonald scored hits on one enemy machine and saw it turn on to its back and dive vertically. Sarre also fired at one, but observed no results. Suddenly he had problems as his Spitfires engine began to misfire. He quickly disengaged from combat and was obliged to force-land his aircraft in a field at Elstead near Ashford in Kent. He stepped out of his Spitfire unhurt.

The pressure of combat was beginning to take its toll on the young pilots of Fighter Command and Sarre was no exception. During combat over London on 7th September, during late afternoon, 603 attacked enemy fighters escorting a bomber formation making for the London docks. Sarre was again the victim of a Me109 and had to bale-out over the Thames. He had been wounded and on landing was taken to hospital. News of his shooting down did not reach Hornchurch or his squadron and he was listed as missing in action for over a day. He was discharged from hospital and returned to Hornchurch on 11th September, to find that some of his personal possessions had been packed up ready to be sent back to his family. In the space of eight days, he had baled out twice and crash-landed twice.

The strain had pushed 'Joey' Sarre to the limit and he was grounded by his commanding officer George Denholm, who could see he was no longer fit for flying duties. He remained with the squadron until 9th November 1940, when he was posted to the Central Flying School at Upavon to become a flying instructor. He remained in this role until the end of the war and was released from the RAF as a flying officer in 1946. Tragically in 1980, 'Joey' Sarre took his own life. Whether this was due to the mental scars of his wartime experiences is not clear; but this brave young pilot who defended our country in its darkest hour is now permanently remembered.

Simpson Road – Wing Commander Peter Simpson DFC*

Peter James Simpson was born at Hove, Sussex on 5th March 1921. No information regarding his early years, but in January 1939, he was granted a short service commission in the Royal Air Force and on completion of flying training, he was sent to No. 11 Group Pool at St Athan in South Wales on 23rd October 1939. Here he went on a conversion course to fly Hawker Hurricane fighter aircraft and was posted to No.111 Squadron based at RAF Acklington on 20th November 1939.

He saw his first combat action over France during the retreat of Allied forces and evacuation at Dunkirk; when on 2nd June 1940, he was able to claim the shooting down of a Messerschmitt 110 fighter-bomber three miles north-west of Dunkirk.

Following the fall of France, his squadron moved to Croydon and was there during the Battle of Britain. Simpson was to shoot down his second enemy aircraft on 19th July, a Messerschmitt 109 over Dover. He was posted away to join No. 64 Squadron at Kenley in early August. The squadron was equipped with Spitfire Mk 1s and Simpson soon made his mark by damaging a Dornier 17 bomber over Chichester 13th August and destroying another Messerschmitt 109 on 16th as well as sharing the destruction of a Heinkel 111 over Tonbridge, Kent. During the engagement his Spitfire was badly damaged by return cannon fire.

He was posted back to 111 Squadron, then based at Debden on the following day and on 18th shot down and probably destroyed a Dornier 17 bomber over Kenley. During his attack on the bomber his own Hurricane received damage and he had to force-land his aircraft close to the clubhouse of the RAC Golf Club at Epsom. Throughout September, Simpson flew continuously and claimed another four enemy aircraft destroyed or damaged. His final victory came on 13th November 1940, after 111 Squadron had withdrawn to Drem, Scotland, when he claimed a third share of a Heinkel 111 seven miles south-east of Aberdeen. He was awarded the Distinguished Flying Cross on 17th December 1940.

During May 1941, he was rested from operations, but returned in December that year to join No. 66 Squadron at Portreath as a newly promoted flight lieutenant. He was given command of his own squadron in July 1942, when he joined No. 130 'Punjab' Squadron based in No. 10 Group covering the area around the south-west of England. Simpson remained here until to January 1943, when he was given a rest period. He was then sent back on operations with No. 504 Squadron in July 1943, as part of the Ibsley Wing before he departed that October. He was promoted to squadron leader on 28th December 1943 and was appointed to be wing leader of the Hornchurch Wing.

During his stay there which was only brief, he was in command of No's 129, 222 and 350 (Belgian) Squadrons. The squadrons had continually been active on escort duty for bomber raids over Northern France as plans for the invasion of Europe where being prepared for 1944. Simpson led the Wing on several occasions, but he was posted from Hornchurch to No. 20 Fighter Wing at Portreath in January 1944 and led its squadrons over the Normandy beaches on D-Day June 6th 1944. He was awarded the Distinguished Service Order on 28th August 1944.

After the end of the war, Simpson remained in the service and became Wing Commander Flying at RAF Tangmere in 1954, where he commanded a Meteor jet squadron and later Hawker Hunter aircraft. He retired from the RAF on 5th March 1968 retaining the rank of group captain. Peter Simpson passed away on 13th November 1987 aged 66.

Sowrey Avenue – Group Captain Frederick Sowrey DSO, MC, AFC

Born at Twigworth in Gloucestershire on 25th August 1893, Frederick Sowrey was one of three sons of John Sowrey, a Deputy Chief Inspector of Inland Revenue. The young Sowrey was educated at home until the age of thirteen; he then won a scholarship to King's College School in Wimbledon, South London where he passed a Bachelor of Science degree. He was still completing his year when the First World War began on 4th August 1914.

He volunteered immediately for army service at the local recruiting office and joined the Royal Fusiliers on 31st August. After completing officer training, he was appointed as a 2nd Lieutenant and posted to France soon after. He took part in the Battle of Loos in 1915 and was wounded and spent the next three months recuperating from his injuries. He was invalided out of the army and decided he would join the Royal Flying Corps, which he did in December 1915.

After undertaking basic flying training and going solo, Sowrey was posted to No.39 Squadron (Home Defence) at Sutton's Farm airfield at Hornchurch in Essex on 17th June 1916; here he struck up friendships with fellow pilots William Leefe-Robinson and Wulstan Tempest who had also only recently joined the squadron. For the next couple of months, the squadron was actively involved in defending the London area against night-attacks by the German airships known as Zeppelins; but they had no success it bringing them down.

However in September 1916, things changed on the night of 2nd/3rd September, Sowrey's colleague William Leefe Robinson was successful in shooting down the first enemy airship over British soil, the SL11 which crashed at Cuffley; Robinson instantly became the hero of the hour and was awarded the Victoria Cross.

On the evening of 23rd September, Freddy Sowrey took off from Sutton's Farm on his evening patrol at 11.30 pm and was ordered to patrol towards Joyce Green, Kent. Flying at a height of 13,000 feet, he sighted a Zeppelin in the far distance at approximately 1.10 am. As he neared the Zeppelin and turned his aircraft towards it, he fired his Lewis gun filled with incendiary bullets from his ammunition magazine into the Zeppelin, and on breaking away from it saw it explode into flame. The giant airship designated as Zeppelin L.32 began to fall slowly at first as the flames began to engulf it, but it speedily fell faster and hit the ground in a field at Snail's Hall Farm, Great Burstead near Billericay. There were no survivors from the German crew.

The next day, hoards of people arrived at the crash-site to get a glimpse of the airship wreckage and Sowrey was also hailed a hero. He was awarded the Distinguished Service Order for his feat, which was gazetted on 4th October 1916.

On 1st December 1916, Sowrey was promoted to the rank of Temporary Captain and appointed as a flight commander in 39 Squadron. Later that year, he was posted to No. 37 Squadron also used in home defence. In 1917, he was sent as a liaison officer over to France and was then transferred to No. 19 Squadron on 14th June 1917, where he flew and achieved twelve enemy aircraft victories over the Western Front from 17th June up till 15th October 1917. Sowrey was awarded the Military Cross to add to his DSO. The citation for his medal read:

For conspicuous gallantry and devotion to duty in shooting down in less than two months, two Albatross scouts and a Rumpler two-seater and a Fokker scout, and in two engagements flying very low and engaging and scattering hostile infantry.

By 1st January 1918, he had been promoted from flight commander to squadron leader; as this was before the changeover in service of the Royal Flying Corps to the Royal Air Force on 1st April 1918; in rank Sowrey was promoted from 2nd Lieutenant (Acting Captain) to Temporary Major. He was then given command of 143 Squadron and remained with them until the end of the war in November 1918.

Sowrey remained in the Royal Air Force after the end of hostilities and was awarded the Air Force Cross on 1st January 1919. He was promoted to wing commander on 1st July 1928 and held various commands including station commander at RAF Northolt before retiring from the service as a group captain on 26th May 1940. One of his son's also named Frederick joined the RAF during the Second World War and went on to become an Air Marshal later during peacetime. Frederick Sowrey died at Eastbourne, Sussex on 21st October 1968

Stapleton Crescent - Air Vice-Marshal Frederick Stapleton CB, DSO, DFC

Frederick Snowden Stapleton was born in Hackney, East London on 4th February 1912 and during his early education excelled academically. He attended the Downing College at Cambridge and gained a Bachelor of Arts award during his time there. He joined the Royal Air Force Volunteer Reserve as a sergeant pilot in 1933, but was awarded a University Commission having learnt to fly at the University Air Squadron and was granted a permanent commission with the rank of pilot officer on 3rd December 1934.

Stapleton was sent to No. 5 Flying Training School and having successfully passed and gained his wings was posted to No.3 Squadron flying Bristol Bulldog biplanes. He was posted away on 8th October 1937 to No. 87 Squadron based at Debden, who had been equipped with the latest RAF Fighter, the Hawker Hurricane. He was promoted quickly and he became an acting flight lieutenant on 3rd March 1938 and made a flight commander in the squadron on 3rd June. He attended a course at the School of Air Navigation in 1939 and in 1940 went on the staff of Headquarters No. 50 Group, Flying Training Command in the Midlands.

He remained there until April 1941, when he was sent to No. 58 Operational Training Unit at Grangemouth, Scotland, to convert on to

Spitfires. Stapleton was posted from here to an operational squadron, No. 54 at RAF Hornchurch as a supernumerary squadron leader. Here, he undertook a number of successful missions with the squadron and on 6th May 1941 claimed his first enemy victory over a Messerschmitt 109 which he downed over Dover. But, he was immediately on the receiving end following this combat and in turn his Spitfire was badly damaged by the German pilot, Major Friedrich Beckh of 4/JG51. Stapleton was able to crash-land his burning Spitfire in a field in Dover and was uninjured.

He was posted from 54 Squadron and moved to 611 Squadron who were also at Hornchurch, as their commanding officer, and with them he was able to claim a third share in a Me109 on 28th May over Calais. During June, he shot down a further two 109s and received notification on 27th June that he was to be promoted to Wing Commander Flying, taking the place of Wing Commander Joe Kyall who had been shot down and was now a prisoner of war.

Leading the Hornchurch Wing, Stapleton's leadership and tactics were put to the test as the Germans put up fierce air resistance as the RAF continued their offensive operations over France, Belgium and Holland. He claimed a further three enemy fighter aircraft between the 4th and 12th July and on 15th received news that he was to be awarded the Distinguished Flying Cross. The citation for his award read:

This officer has led his squadron on almost every operational flight during its recent activities over enemy territory, in which the squadron has destroyed at least twelve enemy aircraft. Two of these were destroyed by Wing Commander Stapleton himself. He has always displayed the utmost enthusiasm to seek out and destroy the enemy and has undoubtedly contributed materially to the successes obtained.

Following the shooting down and capture of Wing Commander Douglas Bader on 9th August 1941, the Hornchurch Wing was tasked with an unusual mission on 19th August, when they were asked to be a Target Support Wing in which they would support six Bristol Blenheim bombers on a raid against Cosnay, and on the way in to the target, they would also drop a new artificial leg for Bader. Unfortunately, due to bad timing the RAF Fighters missed the Blenheims, and became involved in combats with enemy fighters instead. Stapleton leading 611 Squadron engaged some 109s, but none were shot down. However they managed to prevent the Luftwaffe in intercepting the British bombers.

On 12th September, Stapleton assumed command of RAF Hornchurch, when Group Captain Harry Broadhurst went on a well-deserved break for one week. By the 17th September, when he claimed his last enemy aircraft of the war, a Messerschmitt 109 shot down five miles south of Mardyck; Stapleton had a tally of 7 destroyed, 4 and 1 shared probably destroyed and 3 damaged.

He was awarded the Distinguished Service Order medal on 2nd December 1941, which stated:

Since June 1941, this officer has participated in 47 operational sorties. Leading the wing with the utmost coolness and determination, he has taken every opportunity to support the formations and to inflict damage on the enemy. Since being awarded the Distinguished Flying Cross, he has destroyed 4 enemy aircraft and has probably destroyed or damaged several others.

On 3rd December 1941, Frederick Stapleton was posted away from Hornchurch and taken off operational flying and rested before on 23rd February 1942, he became the Chief Instructor of No. 42 Air School at South End, Port Elizabeth in South Africa.

In October, he was made commanding officer at the school and remained in this post until 15th May 1945, when he returned to the United Kingdom as Deputy Director of Operational Requirements. He remained within the RAF during peacetime attending the RAF Staff College in 1947 and becoming Group Captain, Operations at Headquarters Fighter Command in 1948.

In October 1949, he became officer commanding the aerodrome at RAF Linton-on-Ouse and in 1951 was posted to Germany to command RAF Wunsdorf. On 12th January 1956, he was promoted in rank to air commodore and became commander of Northern Sector. He became Senior Air Staff Officer of Headquarters No. 13 Group at the beginning of October 1957 and held this post until he was made the Head of Joint UK Liaison Staff in Australia on 10th February 1959.

His final appointment before retiring from the Royal Air Force in May 1961 was as SASO Transport Command; by which time he had risen to the rank of air vice-marshal. He returned to live in Australia and became Director General of the Manning Company in 1964. He retired from this position on 9th April 1966. Frederick Stapleton died in Australia on 19th April 1974.

Stephen Avenue – Squadron Leader Harbourne Stephen
CBE, DSO, DFC*

Born on 16th April 1916 at Elgin, Morayshire Scotland, Harbourne Mackay Stephen was the son of Thomas Milne Stephen, a banker for the North of Scotland Bank House and a Justice of the Peace and his wife Kathleen Vincent nee Park, who had married at Croydon in 1903. Harbourne was educated firstly at home by a governess up until the age of seven and then attended schools in Elgin, Edinburgh and Shrewsbury. On leaving full-time education his first job was as a copy boy with Allied Newspapers, Grays Inn Road in London in 1931; as he progressed in the industry, he moved up the ladder and was on the advertising staff of the Evening Standard in 1936.

He had a passion for aviation and learnt to fly at weekends at White Waltham aerodrome on Tiger Moth biplanes, and with only nine hours duel instruction, made his first solo flight. He joined the RAF Volunteer Reserve in April 1937 and was given six months absence of leave from his job to train with the regular Royal Air Force.

Stephen was sent to No. 11 Group Fighter Pool at St Athan at the start of September 1939, just as war was declared against Germany; here he converted on to Hawker Hurricane aircraft and was posted on 20th September to join No. 605 Squadron based at Tangmere as a sergeant pilot. On 20th March 1940, he saw his first action against the enemy, when flying as part of Yellow Section they sighted a Heinkel 111 bomber. This was the squadron's first encounter of the war, although they attacked the lone raider, only the section leader claimed any damage on the German and it escaped only to be shot down by aircraft of No. 43 Squadron.

On 1st April 1940, Stephen was commissioned as a pilot officer and was posted to join No. 74 Squadron at Hornchurch on 10th April. It would not be until mid-May that he would see any further action, when the British Army with its back pinned against the French coast was being evacuated from Dunkirk following the German advance that had left the Allies in full retreat. It was on 24th May that Stephen while on patrol over the Dunkirk area, sighted and shared in the shooting down of a German Henschel Hs126 reconnaissance aircraft and also a Dornier 17 bomber. Two days later, he destroyed another HS 126 and on 27th claimed a Messerschmitt 109 and a Dornier 17 that he shared with another pilot.

During this period, he became very good friends with John Mungo-Park and they worked well together as a fighting team. During the Battle of Britain, Stephen was to have his best day against the enemy on 11th August 1940, when during the morning the squadron was scrambled to intercept Messerschmitt 109s over the coast at Dover; Stephen attacked one of the enemy aircraft and fired a burst from his machine guns, sending it plummeting into the sea, he then fired on a second aircraft at close-range and it exploded in mid-air. He then latched on to a third 109 and firing at it saw pieces of the airframe falling away; unfortunately he did not see this machine crash. He finally finished off all of his ammunition on one more enemy aircraft and claimed it as damaged.

Later that day, he was in action once more, this time 12-miles east of Clacton, Essex. Here they encountered a formation of around forty Messerschmitt 110 fighter-bombers. They went into the attack and broke the enemy formation, Stephen was able to get behind one of the Me110s and shoot it down in flames before attacking a second enemy aircraft, which he spent quite a few minutes in chasing and firing his guns, but the German pilot was able to turn his aircraft in various aggressive manoeuvres, before falling to Stephen's guns. He then turned his attentions to another Me110, and scored a number of hits on this before he had to break off his attack, as his ammunition was now spent.

He returned to Manston and re-armed and refuelled, but was ordered aloft ninety minutes later over Margate, where they met a formation of Junkers Ju87 dive-bombers escorted by Me109s. He again shot down a Messerschmitt and saw it dive away and crash in flames, fortunately the German pilot was able to vacate the aircraft and use his parachute. Stephen's final tally of enemy aircraft for that day stood at 3 Me109s destroyed and 1 damaged, 2 Me110s destroyed and 1 damaged, making him an ace and he was awarded the Distinguished Flying Cross on 27th August 1940, with a further award on 15th November of a Bar to his DFC.

Stephen continued to score throughout the remainder of 1940 and was involved with John Mungo-Park while based at Biggin Hill in shooting down the aerodromes 600th enemy aircraft of the war on 30th November 1940, when they brought down a Messerschmitt 109 at an altitude of 34,000 feet, which set a record at that time for air combat. He was recognised further with the Distinguished Service Order on 24th December 1940, rounding off an incredible year in his life.

He was posted from 74 Squadron on 11th January 1941 and sent as a chief flying instructor to No. 59 Operational Training Unit at Turnhouse in Scotland, but was almost immediately ordered to RAF Farnborough to become a test pilot.

He only remained there until June 1941 and longing to get back on operational flying duties, he was posted to No. 130 Squadron at Portreath; in July, Stephen was posted to take command of 234 Squadron at Wittering and while with this unit, he claimed his final two victories of the war, a Ju88 damaged on 12th August near Antwerp and on 15th October 1941, a half share in a Me109 over Le Havre. His final score of enemy aircraft stood at 9 & 8 shared destroyed, 4 and 1 shared unconfirmed destroyed, 3 probables and 7 damaged

Stephen remained with 234 Squadron until early 1942, before he was posted to Jessore, India with the rank of wing commander. He was given command of 166 Fighter Wing in October; based at Chittagong and was involved in halting the Japanese advance, by supporting the Allied ground forces. During one patrol, Stephen was shot down over enemy-held territory and had to parachute down, fortunately he was able to evade capture and return to the Allied lines unscathed. He kept the parachute and later had it made into a silk dressing gown.

During 1943, he was posted on to the staff of Lord Louis Mountbatten's Headquarters, 224 Group Fighter Operations at Kandy, Ceylon and he remained in the Far East for the remainder of the war. With hostilities over, he was offered a permanent commission within the Royal Air Force, but he declined wishing to return and take-up and offer given to him by Lord Beaverbrook to join the Express Newspaper Empire. He married Erica Palmer in 1947; they had met in Ceylon where she was serving in the Women's Royal Naval Service.

Stephen worked for the Scottish Daily Express, Scottish Sunday Express and Evening Citizen during the late 1940s and into the 1950s, and had risen to general manager by 1955. He became general manager of the Sunday Express 1958 and the Sunday Graphic by 1960. In 1963 he moved to the Daily Telegraph to become the assistant managing director, but within several weeks was promoted to managing director of the company, which he held until 1986.

He was awarded the CBE in 1985 and on retirement he lived the rest of his life at Newbury, Berkshire. He died age 85 years on 20th August 2001

Tempest Way – Major Wulstan Tempest DSO, MC, MiD

Born on 22nd January 1891 at home at Ackworth Grange, Pontefract, Yorkshire, Wulstan Joseph Tempest was one of three sons and two sisters of parents Wilfrid and Florence Helen Tempest nee O'Rourke. His father was chairman of the West Riding Bench of the Pontefract Division. Wulstan was educated at Stonyhurst, where he won a distinction in mathematics and then spent three years in the navy as a cadet on the training ship 'Worcester.' From there he took up employment in mining engineering and spent three months in South Africa sugar farming. Before the outbreak of the First World War, he and his brother Edmund went to Canada in 1911 and ran a farm estate in Saskatchewan.

When war was declared in August 1914, both he and his brother returned to Britain to join the fight. Tempest joined the King's Own Yorkshire Light Infantry as an officer and saw action in Flanders in October 1915. He was wounded during the first Battle of Ypres after being buried in a dugout hit by artillery fire. He was sent back to England to recuperate and served with a garrison battalion before he was transferred to join the Royal Flying Corps. After learning to fly and gaining his wings he became a flying officer on 17th June 1916 and was posted to No.39 (Home Defence) Squadron at Sutton's Farm, Hornchurch.

Here, he became good friends with fellow officers Frederick Sowrey and William Leefe-Robinson. The squadron was at readiness during this period against the night attacks by German airships, who attempted to bomb towns and cities across the south-east of England. Both Leefe-Robinson and Frederick Sowrey achieved success against two of the raiders during September 1916.

On the night of 1st/2nd October, Tempest was evidently having an evening meal with a lady friend at Epping, when he received the call that he was to get airborne immediately following an airship raid alert. Taking off in his BE2c biplane, he sighted the giant Zeppelin L32 over Hertfordshire and gained height in pursuit of the raider. During the flight, his own aircraft caused him problems, having a broken fuel pump, which required him to prime the engine by hand. He managed to get into a position to open fire on the Zeppelin and after only firing his machine gun in a single pass; he managed to set alight the German machine. It quickly became a flaming pyre and started to fall to earth, finally crashing at Potters Bar; there were no survivors from the crew.

Tempest headed home for Hornchurch and through total fatigue by having to pump his fuel into the engine, he crashed his aircraft on landing. He stepped from his biplane with only a minor gash to his head.

The following day, Tempest travelled to the scene of total devastation where the Zeppelin had crashed at Oakmere Park, Potters Bar. He evidently, was too modest to tell the soldiers who guarded the crash-site that he was the airman who had shot the Zeppelin down and he paid a shilling like everyone else to view the scene.

For his action in bringing down the Zeppelin, Tempest was awarded the Distinguished Service Order and also hailed as a hero along with his two friends Robinson and Sowrey.

He remained with the squadron until early 1917, when he was posted to No. 100 Squadron in early 1917 and was gazetted as being Mentioned in Despatches on 25th January 1917 'for services rendered in connection with the war.'

Tempest took part in a bombing raid on 29th/30th April 1917 against German targets in Northern France and was awarded the Military Cross on 18th October for his actions during subsequent raids that had followed, after recommendations for gallantry were sent from Headquarters 1st Brigade to Headquarters Royal Flying Corps on 9th September 1917. The citation for his Military Cross stated the following:

For conspicuous gallantry, and devotion to duty on many occasions. He has successfully bombed railway sidings and aerodromes, often in mist and cloudy weather and at low altitudes, causing much damage to his objectives. On one occasion, he descended to a very low height and dropped bombs on two moving trains, causing them both to derail. This officer has taken part in 34 night-bombing raids.

Wulstan Tempest ended the war with the rank of Major and retired to civilian life. When the Second World War started in September 1939, Tempest returned to command the Newbury Home Guard during the rest of the war. It is believed he did return to live in Canada, but this author cannot clarify this. He died in 1966 aged 75 years.

Tuck Road – Wing Commander Robert Stanford Tuck, DSO, DFC* DFC (US)

Robert Roland Stanford Tuck was born in Catford, London on 1st July 1916 the second son of Jewish parents Stanley Lewis and Ethel Clara Tuck and was educated at the St. Dunstan's Preparatory School and College, Reading in Berkshire and finished there in 1932. He joined the Merchant Navy and was employed by the marine company of Lamport and Holt as a cadet and went to sea. He worked aboard the company's refrigerator ship, the 'Marconi' and travelled extensively. It was on board the ship that he learnt the use of a rifle and would often target passing Sharks close to the vessel.

In 1935, Tuck was on leave from his work in the navy, when he noticed an advert in a newspaper asking for young fit men to join the Royal Air Force. He immediately wrote off for an application and received notification to be interviewed and after taking medical and written examinations, appeared before a selection board and was soon after accepted for flight training with the temporary rank of pilot officer. He was sent to RAF Uxbridge on 16th September 1935, where he undertook basic drill and lectures before being sent to No. 3 Flying Training School at Grantham in Lincolnshire. There he learnt to fly on Avro Tutor biplanes and after a few weeks and 13-hours of duel-instruction; he went solo on 24th October 1935. It was not until

August 5th 1936; that he was posted to his first operational squadron, joining No. 65 Squadron based at RAF Hornchurch, Essex.

Here, Tuck flew the Gloster Gauntlet and Gladiator biplanes and became part of the squadrons aerobatic display team. One pilot who remembers Tuck during this period was Brian Kingcome, he recalls Tuck as 'a brilliant pilot, but not everybody's friend as he was a bit flamboyant and thought by some as not enough stiff upper lip; too much the Clark Gable type with pencil thin moustache, which was illegal according to RAF regulations.'

Fate would take a hand in Tuck's future, when 18th January 1938, while practising aerobatics with two other pilots in the team, tragedy struck, when Sergeant Gaskell's aircraft hit turbulence and reared up in front of Bob Tuck's biplane and his propeller sliced through Gaskell's cockpit killing him. Tuck's own Gloster Gauntlet wings began to crumple and he tried to free himself from the cockpit, which he managed to do after a struggle. He floated down to earth by parachute, but noticed blood gushing from his right cheek; he had been slashed across his face by a bracing wire from the aircraft's wing. He landed and was immediately taken to hospital and treated. He spent six days there recovering from the accident which left him a permanent scar.

He returned to flying duties and continued in the aerobatic team only to have a similar accident occur, when he and Flying Officer Leslie Bicknell collided over Brentwood in April 1938, both pilots parachuted to safety this time.

In December 1938, Tuck was chosen to be one of the first RAF pilots to be trained on the new Spitfire aeroplane. He was sent to RAF Duxford to learn all aspects of the new aircraft under the direction of Supermarine test pilot Jeffery Quill.

At the outbreak of war, Tuck was still with 65 Squadron and flew many patrols covering the defence of the south-east of England. He was posted away from 65 Squadron on 1st May 1940 to join No. 92 Squadron as a flight commander at Croydon and saw his first action over Dunkirk later that month. The squadron moved to Hornchurch to undertake operations over France during the evacuation at Dunkirk and it was during one of these patrols that he claimed his first success against the enemy on 23rd May, when he shot down three Messerschmitt 110s and probably destroyed a 109.

The following day, he claimed two Dornier bombers and added another five further aircraft to his score by 2nd June. For his actions over Dunkirk he was awarded the Distinguished Flying Cross, which he received from King George IV at Hornchurch on 27th June 1940. The citation for the award read:

During May 1940, this officer led his flight in company with his squadron on two offensive patrols over Northern France. As a result of one of these patrols in which the squadron engaged a formation of some 60 aircraft, the squadron commander was later reported missing, and the flight commander wounded and in hospital. Flight Lieutenant Tuck assumed command and on the following day led the squadron consisting of only eight aircraft, on a further patrol engaging an enemy formation of fifty aircraft. During these engagements the squadron has shot down ten enemy aircraft and possibly another twenty-four. Throughout the combats, this officer has displayed great dash and gallantry.

He remained with 92 Squadron during the months of July and August 1940, flying from Pembury in South Wales and then Biggin Hill in Kent. On 18th August, he chased two Junkers Ju88s back across the Channel on their way back from a bombing raid and was able to shoot one down, unfortunately his own Spitfire was hit by enemy fire and part of his propeller blade was shot away and he suffered damage to the oil and coolant tank.

Tuck was able to fly his aircraft back over English soil before the engine finally packed up and he had no option but to parachute to safety. He was at very low altitude and his parachute only just opened in time before he hit the ground. He suffered a wrenched leg on landing and was helped immediately, having landed in the grounds of the estate of Lord Cornwallis at Hornsmonden, Kent. Tuck was given tea by Cornwallis before he was transported back to his squadron.

On 11th September, he received news that he was to be given command of his own squadron, No. 257; they were equipped with Hawker Hurricanes and based at Martlesham Heath in Suffolk and he led them into action on many occasions. His own score of enemy aircraft destroyed continued to rise and by 25th October, he had been awarded a second Bar to his DFC and on 7th January 1941, received a further award of the Distinguished Service Order.

Tuck was leading the squadron on 21st June, when on an offensive sweep over the Channel, he was able to claim two Messerschmitt 109s in succession, but he in turn was shot down by one of the German fighters and had to bale-out into the sea. Fortunately, he inflated his own small one-man dinghy and was picked up out of the cold waters by a coal barge from Gravesend and brought ashore.

In July 1941, he was appointed Wing Leader at RAF Duxford and during his time there accounted for three more of the enemy. That October, he was chosen to go to the United States on a liaison trip with five other RAF officers, where they undertook a series of lectures and flew American aircraft of various types. Tuck returned to Britain in December 1942 and was given the role of Wing Leader at Biggin Hill.

On 28th January 1942, he led the Wing on a raid against the alcohol distillery at Hesdin, twenty miles inland from Le Touquet. Having reached the target and setting the place aflame, they continued inland and Tuck noticed a steam engine and dived down to attack it, the steam engine exploded in a mass of steam and smoke, but on clearing the debris, Tuck was hit by German 20mm and 37mm anti-aircraft guns. His Spitfire was hit in the engine and at once belched black smoke and oil covered his canopy's front screen. Tuck was too low to use his parachute, so had no option but to crash-land. On landing, he was immediately captured by the Germans and was sent the next day to a Dulag transit camp near Leipzig in Germany, before eventually going to Stalag Luft III prison camp at Sagan. Here he tried numerous attempts to escape before being sent to another camp called Belaria, which was situated six miles from Sagan in late 1943.

Tuck remained in this camp until January 1945, when he along with the rest of the prisoners were sent on the long march west by the Germans, who were now retreating from the advancing Russians. On reaching the village of Bransdorf in Upper Silesia, Tuck and a Polish pilot, Zbishek Kustrzynski made their attempt for freedom by hiding under a pile of straw in an old barn, while their fellow captors were herded out to continue the march. They were not detected and were able to evade the Germans and make their way to the Russian lines. Tuck and his comrade finally made their way to the Black Sea and boarded a liner 'The Duchess of Richmond.'

On return to Britain at war's end, Bob Tuck continued to serve in the RAF until 13th May 1949. His wartime score of enemy aircraft stood at 27 and 2 shared destroyed, 1 and 1 unconfirmed destroyed, 6 probables and 6 and 1 shared damaged. He married and became a mushroom farmer, living in Sandwich, Kent. He died on 5th May 1987 aged 70 years.

Wells Gardens – Group Captain Edward Preston Wells
DSO, DFC*

Born at Cambridge, New Zealand on 26th July 1917, the son of a farmer, he was always known to family and friends as 'Bill.' He was educated at the local high school and continued to work in farming. He was an excellent 12-bore shotgun marksman especially using deflection shooting and won many local competitions; because of this he earned the name of 'Hawkeye.' Wells had an interest in aviation and applied for a short service commission within the Royal New Zealand Air Force in October 1938 and was successful and accepted into the service in mid-April 1939.

He was called up on 26th October 1939 and sent to the Ground Training School at Weraroe. From there he was sent to No. 2 Flying Training School at New Plymouth before going to another Flying Training School at Woodbourne on 15th January 1940 and with his training completed, he boarded the vessel RMS 'Rangitata' on 7th June and set sail for Britain.

Soon after his arrival, Wells was sent to No. 7 Operational Training Unit at Hawarden on 4th August 1940, to convert on to Spitfire aircraft. He was posted to join No. 266 Squadron at RAF Wittering in Cambridgeshire on 26th. He flew with the squadron, but did not achieve any victories during his time with them, and was posted away to No. 41 Squadron at Hornchurch on 2nd October 1940.

It was with this squadron that he claimed his first victories of the war, destroying a Messerschmitt 109 on 17th October and probably destroying another and damaging one further on 29th October. During November, Wells continued to add to his tally by destroying a Me109 on 2nd November and when the Italian Air Force made a token attack against Britain on 11th, he was the first pilot to sight and intercept the Fiat CR 42 fighters and shot one down over Ordfordness and probably destroyed a Henschel Hs 126. His last victim for that year was a Messerschmitt 109 on 27th November 1940, shot down between Chatham and Dover.

Still flying with 41 Squadron, he continued into the next year by claiming a half-share in the destruction of a Heinkel bomber south-west of Clacton, Essex.

During March 1941, a new all New Zealand fighter squadron was formed at Driffield and Flying Officer Wells joined it on 15th of that month. He claimed the squadron's first victory on 5th July, when 452 were detailed to act as escort on a raid to Lille by Short Stirling bombers. Wells destroyed a Me109 during this operation and another on 24th, and received the well-earned award of a Distinguished Flying Cross on 7th August 1941. The citation for the medal stated:

This officer has served with fighter squadrons since May 1940 and has taken part in many engagements against the enemy. He has destroyed at least 5 of their aircraft and has damaged others. He has at all times shown the greatest courage and determination.

'Hawkeye' Wells steadily increased his score within the next four months, destroying a further four of the enemy up till November 1941, all of them German fighter aircraft. He had completed forty-six missions over enemy held territory and was awarded a Bar to his DFC and was given command of 485 Squadron on 22nd November.

On 12th February 1942, his squadron was ordered airborne, when the German battle-cruisers Scharnhorst and Gneisenau tried to escape through the English Channel from the French port at Brest, and make their way to the German port of Wilhelmshaven.

Wells squadron was ordered to engage the Luftwaffe fighter screen that had been placed above the German ships as protection. He found no fighter aircraft to attack, so attacked an E-boat that was acting as escort. They strafed the E-boat and left it sinking in mid-Channel.

On 5th May, he was promoted to acting wing commander and posted as Wing Leader at RAF Kenley, Surrey. Leading from the front, he claimed two more enemy aircraft destroyed during May and June, before he was awarded a well-earned Distinguished Service Order on 28th July 1942 and given a rest period. He was sent back to

New Zealand, and offered a very important job, but he rejected the proposal, wishing instead to return to operational flying. He came back in March 1943, via the United States and while there visited aircraft factories and spoke with the workers giving moral lifting talks.

On return to England, he was sent on a course at the RAF Staff College and on completion was able to return to lead the Kenley Wing until that November. He was then posted on the staff at No. 11 Group Fighter Command Headquarters, as Wing Commander Training, but he was not happy in this role, finding it tedious. He was lucky enough to be able to return to operational flying, when he was offered the job of becoming the leader of the Tangmere Wing in March 1944, which was equipped with the latest Spitfires. On 20th March, he was able to destroy a Messerschmitt 410 fighter he had caught on the ground.

He led the Wing on numerous occasions during the build-up to D-Day and was also given command of both the Detling and West Malling Wings. Having been flying since March, he was rested again and sent to the RAF's Central Fighter Establishment at Wittering to command the Day Fighter Leader's School, where he remained until the end of the war.

He was offered a permanent commission following the end of hostilities and remained in the RAF until 1960. He had met and married Mary de Booy a Dutch girl in 1943; she had escaped with her parents and sister from the Nazis in 1940 and they had met at a tea dance in London, when she worked for the Red Cross. They had a son and a daughter. Wells returned to farming and settled in Woodbridge, before moving to Spain to become an expert in sub-tropical fruits, which he gathered from all corners of the world. He won many awards from the Spanish authorities for his work in this field.

He returned to Britain following the death of his wife in 2001 and he passed away on 1st November 2005 aged 88

BIBLIOGRAPHY

The following books are recommended by the author as essential background and reference reading for those interested in RAF Hornchurch or the pilots listed in this book

Aces High, Christopher Shores and Clive Williams, Grub Street 1994

Al Deere, wartime fighter pilot-peacetime commander, Richard C. Smith, Grub Street, 2003

Battle of Britain Then and Now Mk V, Winston Ramsey, After the Battle 1980

Fighter Command's Sergeant Aces of 1940, Richard C. Smith, Mitor Publications, 2007

Fighter Squadrons in the Battle of Britain, Anthony Robinson, Arms & Armour 1987

Fighter Squadrons of the RAF, John Rawlings, MacDonald & Co 1969

Fly for your Life, Larry Forrester, Frederick Muller Ltd, 1956

Hornchurch Scramble, the Definitive History, Richard C. Smith, Grub Street 2000

Hornchurch Offensive, Richard C. Smith, Grub Street, 2001

Hornchurch Eagles, Richard Smith, Grub Street, 2002

Keith Park, Vincent Orange, Grub Street, 2001

Men of the Battle of Britain, Kenneth Wynn, Gliddon Books 1989

Nine Lives, Alan Deere, Wingham Press Ltd 1992

Paddy Finucane Fighter Ace, Doug Stokes, William Kimber & Co Ltd 1983

Raiders Approach, H.T. Sutton, Gale & Polden 1956

Richard Hillary, the Definitive Biography, David Ross, Grub Street, 2000

Sky Tiger, The story of Sailor Malan, Norman Franks, William Kimber & Co-Ltd, 1980

Spitfire into Battle, W. Duncan-Smith, John Murray Ltd, 1981

Spitfires over Japan, Dorothy Bouchier, Global Oriental Ltd, 2005

Tigers, The story of 74 Squadron, Bob Cossey, Arms & Armour, 1992
The Air Battle of Dunkirk, Norman Franks, Grub Street, 2000
The Greatest Squadron of Them All, History of 603 Squadron, David Ross, Bruce Blanche and William Simpson, Grub Street, 2003
The Last Enemy, Richard Hillary, MacMillan & Co Ltd, 1942

Back Cover Photographs: Pilots are named as follows in clockwise direction:

Squadron Leader Ronald Berry
Flight Lieutenant Alan Deere with Colin Gray
Wing Commander Harry Broadhurst
Sergeant Alfred Sarre
Flight Lieutenant Eric Lock
Flying Officer Richard Hillary
Lieutenant Wulstan Tempest
Squadron Leader James Leathart
Lieutenants Frederick Sowrey with William Leefe Robinson
Wing Commander Edward 'Hawkeye' Wells
Flight Lieutenant John Mungo Park with H.M. Stephen
Squadron Leader Robert Stanford Tuck
Flying Officer Peter Pease
Wing Commander 'Paddy' Finucane

For further information regarding purchasing books or DVDs on RAF Hornchurch or other aviation books published by Mitor Publications visit the website at: www.mitorpublications.co.uk